ASCENSION
TRAINING

Don Durrett

(Third Edition, August 2023)

Copyright © 2015 by Donald David Durrett
All rights reserved.

ISBN: 978-1-4276-5549-3

WWW.DONDURRETT.COM

Books by Don Durrett

A Stranger From the Past

Conversations With an Immortal

Finding Your Soul

Finding Your Soul Workbook

New Thinking for the New Age

Spirit Club

Last of the Gnostics

The Gathering

The Way

Team Creator

The Path Forward

Get Healthy / Stay Healthy

America's Political Cold War

Post America: A New Constitution

The Demise of America

You will know the truth,
and the truth will set you free.

— *John 8:32*

Contents

Introduction iii

Chapter One
Near-Death Experience 1

Chapter Two
The Meetup Group 17

Chapter Three
Planetary Ascension 33

Chapter Four
Julie's House 51

Chapter Five
The Future 63

Chapter Six
Three Systems 79

Chapter Seven
God's Virtues 89

Chapter Eight
The Truth Shall Set You Free 103

Chapter Nine
Ascension Training 119

Chapter Ten
Our Mindset-The Final Step to Ascension 133

Introduction

This book is a fictional story, although it could very well come true. Perhaps not as I have portrayed it, but something similar. There will be people like Johnny, the lead character, who find out the truth about planetary ascension and attempt to share it with the world.

The planet is currently in the process of ascending to a higher frequency, a higher vibration. This has huge implications. For highly evolved souls, they will have the potential to literally disappear and ascend to a higher dimension. For those who remain, the meaning of life will become known to all. This will lead to peace on earth and a humanity-based civilization.

We are literally going to experience a shift in consciousness. It is unknown when it will occur. Our spirit messengers keep saying, "Very soon," but they won't give us a date. It could be a few years or perhaps even a decade from now. I'm 55 and I came to experience this shift, so we are getting close. The pages you are about to read will give you an understanding of what is about to happen. It can also be used as a guide for ascension training.

One final thought. I highly recommend that you read this book twice. The first time to expose yourself to the concepts. The second time to learn them. It is one of my favorite books and is loaded with information.

Don Durrett 8/8/2023

Chapter One

NEAR-DEATH EXPERIENCE

Johnny appeared to be a normal kid. He was fourteen and a freshman in high school. His friends were ordinary and stayed out of trouble. They did their homework and played video games when they had time on their hands. None of them took drugs or drank alcohol. They were good kids from good families in the affluent community of Walnut Creek, California. The only thing they really had in common was they didn't like sports. They had no desire to kick a ball, hit a ball, or throw a ball. Instead, they preferred to stay out of the limelight.

Johnny was a closet anarchist. He thought society was dysfunctional and that government and corporations were destroying the world. He wanted the world to be a better place, but he had no idea how to help it. At the dinner table, he was constantly asking his parents questions about society. His sister, who was a year younger, would roll her eyes at his constant barrage of questions. When she got frustrated, she would say, "Who cares?"

Most children stop asking questions around five or six years of age. Not Johnny. He seemed to be full of questions, most of them pertaining to humanity and how society was organized to help people live. Johnny's parents never understood where these questions came from and, when he was younger, almost took him to a psychologist. They decided against it because his questions seemed to be logical, and they thought he would outgrow it.

If there was a theme to his questions, it would be, "Why are we here?" and "Why are we living like we do?" Johnny was searching for answers and wanted to know why he was alive and what was his role in society. Normally, these are questions that some adults asked themselves, but Johnny had been doing it all of his life.

* * * * *

Johnny never saw it coming. He was riding his bike to school one day and a car slammed into him, causing him to fly ten feet through the air, crashing onto the pavement. The impact of the car caused him to nearly lose consciousness, but the collision with the pavement cracked his helmet and knocked him out cold.

His heart stopped and he lay dead in the street. The ambulance arrived ten minutes later, and it appeared to be hopeless to save his life. The paramedics applied CPR and, incredibly, he started breathing. At the hospital, they found he had a broken arm, fractured ribs, a severe concussion, and an assortment of contusions and bruises. Amazingly, he had no internal injuries.

When his parents walked in to see him, they were surprised by the smile on his face and the joy in his expression. He had to have been in severe pain, but that did not seem to diminish his attitude.

"I found all of the answers!" he exclaimed.

"Johnny," his father implored, "please calm down. You need to rest. Save your energy."

"No, you don't understand," Johnny exclaimed. "I'm going to be fine. I get to tell the world the answers. It's going to be a better place."

"Johnny," his mother said, "we will talk later. For now, please just rest."

Johnny wanted to talk now, but his parents clearly were not in the mood. He put his head back on the pillow and relaxed. He wondered if they even cared about what he had just experienced. The next day when they came back, he decided to remain silent and

Chapter One : Near-Death Experience

see if his parents asked him about what he was so excited about the day before. Instead, they were only interested in his health.

He stayed in the hospital for three days until the doctors were sure his concussion was no longer a threat to his health. Once he got home, he needed to rest for another month for his ribs to heal. He spent this time writing down what he experienced when he died. At the dinner table, he stopped asking questions. Instead, he seemed to be urgently eating his food so that he could get back to his writing.

After a few days of this routine, his dad went into his room and asked what he was writing about.

"Perhaps you should get Mom, so that I don't have to repeat it to both of you."

His father nodded and then came back into the room with his mother.

"Do you remember the day of the accident, when you came into my hospital room and I said that I found all of the answers?"

They both nodded, a bit puzzled by his serious demeanor.

"Well, I did," Johnny said. "Ask me something about your soul, or the meaning of life."

His parents looked at each other, stunned.

Johnny's dad spoke. "Before I ask you that, can you explain where these answers came from?"

"I can try," Johnny said, "but it will be difficult for you to comprehend. The simplest way I can explain it is that I was downloaded with knowledge to share with the world. After the accident, my soul left my body and I was taken by an ascended master to another dimension. It was an amazing place and I wanted to stay there, but he told me I had to go back into my body. Before I left, he offered to give me the answers I was searching for. He told me I could have them, but it was a gift that I had to share with the world."

Johnny paused to see if his parents believed him. They seemed to be listening intently, so he continued. "He then asked me if I wanted this burden. I told him, 'More than anything!' He smiled and then downloaded the information."

"Can you describe some of it?" his mother asked.

Johnny smiled. "Oh yeah. That's what I have been writing down. It's basically the meaning of life."

Johnny's dad raised his eyebrows. "Can you explain it? The meaning of life?"

"Yes. It's really simple, yet really, really hard to achieve. The simple part is knowing why we are here. This planet is not real, it's a temporary illusion. It's temporal and not permanent. It's created for one purpose, to act as a stage, a setting, where souls can evolve and become aware of who they are...."

Johnny paused, wondering if he should tell them, but decided they couldn't handle the truth.

"So, the simple part is that life, or more specifically, a lifetime in a physical body, is to evolve the soul. Everyone on this planet is here for a specific reason. And that reason is unique to that soul.

"One lifetime, one incarnation, is actually only a blip of experience for the soul. The true objective of life is much bigger than one lifetime. What we are each trying to achieve is what can be called enlightenment, or spiritual awareness. This can only be achieved by evolving the soul to the level of awareness where you understand who you are."

"You lost me," his mother said.

Johnny smiled. "It can get complex. Let me explain. When you leave your body after this lifetime, you will go back to the same place that you were at before you incarnated. It will act like a magnet and pull you right back. At this location, you will plan your next incarnation in order to evolve. Once you evolve to the level of an ascended master, you no longer have to return to the same place and plan your next life. Instead, you are free to do as

Chapter One : Near-Death Experience

you wish. Free to evolve on your own. You will have evolved to the point where you no longer require guidance. Until then, you are locked on the wheel of karma, requiring guidance from ascended masters and other highly evolved souls."

Johnny's dad laughed. "You make it sound like we are children and we can't leave home until we are mature enough."

Johnny smiled. "That's a good analogy. Until the soul is mature enough, it is not allowed the freedom to make mischief."

Johnny's mom was skeptical. "Are you saying that everyone on this planet is here to evolve their soul, so that they can become ascended masters?"

Johnny nodded. "And that's the really hard part. It's not easy to achieve. It can take thousands of lifetimes. Once you become an ascended master, you can do anything and you can become anything. There are literally no limitations. We can evolve to the point where we can create life itself. We are all literally gods in the making. It will make your mind spin if you think about it deeply.

"Jesus was an ascended master, and we can become one, too. Normally, this wouldn't be possible, but the planet is ascending, making it possible for nearly everyone to advance rapidly if they apply themselves."

Johnny's dad grinned. "I want to believe you, Johnny, but it doesn't make any sense. You are implying that this planet is basically a school for gods in the making, yet everyone is oblivious to this fact. Not only that, but the vast majority of people are nowhere close to sainthood, or what you call an ascended master. How could everyone be a god in the making?"

Johnny hesitated to reply. He wasn't sure if he should tell them the truth, that they were God. That there was only one consciousness, which we all shared. He decided they couldn't handle it. "All I can do is share what I know. If you don't want to believe me, there is nothing I can do to change your mind. But this is my mission in life, and I will be sharing this information with the world."

His parents were silent, a bit stunned at what had happened to their son. They turned and walked out.

Johnny was glad that he didn't tell them the truth about who they were, or talk about planetary ascension and where society is heading. They would have thought he was crazy. From now on, he wouldn't be talking with his parents about spiritual topics. He would keep his conversations with them directed toward society in general. He still had questions about how society was organized, and both of his parents were well-versed in this area.

* * * * *

After a couple of months of writing, Johnny decided to start a blog and a YouTube channel. He called them both The Meaning of Life Explained. He started posting his writing on his blog. On weekends when he had more time, he would create videos and post them to his YouTube channel. The videos sometimes were more than 30 minutes long. They were generally comprised of Johnny looking into his laptop camera and explaining the meaning of life and planetary ascension.

Soon word leaked to the local *CNBS News* affiliate that a local fourteen-year-old had a near-death experience and had begun blogging about the meaning of life. They came knocking on his door asking for an interview.

"Is Johnny home?" the reporter asked. "I'm a reporter with *CNBS*."

The reporter was wearing a press credential and a cameraman was standing behind her. Their van had a *CNBS* sign painted on the side.

Chapter One : Near-Death Experience

Johnny's mother hesitated, not wanting her son to be exposed to something that could harm him psychologically. He had been through enough already.

"I'm home!" Johnny shouted as he ran to the door. He was excited that he could do an interview and get the word out.

His mother relented and opened the door. "Come in," she said.

"Follow me," Johnny said. "We can do the interview in my room."

He let the reporter and cameraman into his room and then closed the door.

"My parents aren't too excited about my newly found knowledge," he grinned. "It's better if we keep the door closed."

The cameraman was already clipping a microphone to Johnny's shirt.

"If you sit there," the reporter said, pointing to a chair, "that's probably the best place."

Johnny laughed. "Sorry, we don't have a lot of choices."

"No worries," the reporter said. "We can make it work."

She looked over at the cameraman. "Are you ready?"

"Almost," he said, positioning the tripod with the camera attached.

She smiled at Johnny. "Are you ready to do an interview?"

"Oh yeah," he said. "I've been hoping for an opportunity."

"Okay, I'm ready," the cameraman said.

She looked at Johnny. "We'll roll the camera and I'll start asking you questions. Back at the studio we will do the introduction and shots of me asking you questions. For now, the camera will stay on you the entire interview. Are you ready to begin?"

Johnny nodded.

"Let's start at the beginning. Can you describe your near-death experience?"

"I was hit by a car and clinically dead for about ten minutes. During that time, I left my body and was taken to another dimension by an advanced soul. He asked me if I wanted the answers that I had been searching for. Such as, why are we here? And what is the meaning of life?

"I said yes, and he downloaded a large amount of information from his mind into mine. It was nearly instantaneously transferred, but afterward, I could tell you in great detail why we are on this planet.

"Before he gave me the information, he said that it would be both a gift and a burden, and that I had to take both if I wanted the information. Also, he told me that I had to share the gift with the world. I agreed."

"What did he look like?" the reporter asked.

"It's not really relevant, because I can't describe him accurately. He didn't look like us, because the dimension was a much different reality. From a conceptual standpoint, he looked like a wise old man, but the density of his form was not solid."

She nodded. "And what did he tell you?"

"It's not what he told me, but what he gave me. He transferred a large amount of knowledge into my mind."

"Such as?" she asked.

"Everyone on this planet is here to learn lessons, except those few rare ascended masters who are here to help us. Everyone else came for the explicit reason of expanding the knowledge of their soul. Everyone is here to learn lessons that are possible through experience. Without experience, the soul remains in stasis. Although, since we are eternal beings, it's not necessarily a bad thing to be in stasis.

"However, most souls choose to grow and expand. That's why we expose ourselves to hardships and difficulty. We do it to grow, and there is a level of awareness that we are all trying to obtain. Once we reach a certain level, we are then free to go our own way

Chapter One : Near-Death Experience

and teach ourselves. Until we reach this level, we are stuck on the wheel of karma, constantly trying to get off. It is a very difficult undertaking."

"So, you are saying that reincarnation is real?" she asked.

Johnny nodded. "Yes, in fact, it takes thousands of lifetimes to get off the wheel, or become an ascended master. Until you have advanced to the level of an ascended master, you must go back to your group. Everyone on the wheel belongs to a certain group. Once you leave your body, you will immediately return to your home base. It acts like a magnet that pulls you home.

"Once you're back at your home base, you plan your next lifetime or series of lifetimes. This planning is all done with the intent of growing the awareness of the soul, until you have reached the level of an ascended master. At that time, you will be free to go your own way, without the need of spiritual guidance."

"Is this essentially the meaning of life?" she asked.

Johnny nodded. "It is exactly the meaning of life. We are here to grow and expand the awareness of the soul. The soul has unlimited potential. However, to tap into this potential, it must be matured and honed. The process is very meticulous and extremely difficult. For instance, it generally takes more than a thousand lifetimes to become an ascended master. No one can do it quickly."

The reporter was intrigued. "If increasing spiritual awareness is the meaning of life, is there a way to speed up the process?"

Johnny nodded. "Yes, but it is not easy. There are many ways. I'm currently using what I call the hand prayer, although it is more precisely the five-finger prayer. Each morning when I get up, I do a prayer and try to hold that energy all day. I begin with my thumb. The thumb represents who I serve. Do I serve my ego, or do I serve my soul? The index finger represents a choice of where I am going to point my focus: gratitude or pride. If I am grateful, then I will serve the soul. If I am prideful, then I will serve the ego. The middle finger represents integrity and virtue. The extent of my integrity and virtue will determine how I serve. The ring finger represents unconditional love and trust. This is obtained by accepting everything that happens with neutrality and gratitude. Everything is a blessing, and everything is an opportunity. By trusting that everything is happening for a purpose, I can maintain a frequency of love. I can trust that the heart-center will not lead me astray. Finally, the pinky is how I stay in the heart-center. The tiny pinky reminds me not to be prideful slash ego-oriented, but instead, to stay in the heart-center and serve humanity by being grateful, trusting, and connected to everything."

"Are you saying that eliminating the ego is key to spiritual awareness?"

Johnny was quick to reply. "Not eliminating it, but marginalizing it enough so that it does not impinge on our connection to our soul. Our ego-identity is false. It is our monkey-brain that thinks it knows. We have to get out of our head and connected to our heart-center, which is our soul. For instance, when I had an NDE, and left my body, my consciousness came with me. My brain did not, yet I was still intelligent and knew how I was. That intelligence needs to lead us. That intelligence is in the heart-center, and not in our heads. That is where wisdom is found. That is where our real self is found. The ego is just trying to confuse us of what is real. It is what Mary Magdalene tried to tell us. The ego is the mischief-maker. The ego does not come with us when we leave this lifetime. The soul does. So, we need to focus on the soul, which is the real self."

"So, it is our real self that we are trying to turn into?"

Johnny smiled. "Exactly, and it is found within. It is found in the heart, what the Gnostics called the Nous."

The reporter was skeptical. "How does the devil play into all of this?"

Johnny hesitated, contemplating his answer. "First of all, there is nothing separate from the Creator. Separation is a lie. Separation is an illusion. I don't believe in the devil, but if he exists, then he is another persona of the Creator. Evil, on the other hand, does exist. But it is nothing more than another face of the Creator. We are all facets of the Creator. Everything is one and there is no separation from the Creator. Trying to distinguish God from the devil misses the point of life. We are each on our own, and if we find our way, then evil cannot find us. Evil is a pathway that can only be found by those who are astray. This is why evil is live spelled backwards. If we are living in a positive manner, then there is no reason to fear evil. Evil is attracted to you from your belief in separation.

"This is called co-resonance. What you damn through judgment, you attract to yourself. This is God's way of teaching us. Conversely, you set yourself free by loving yourself and blessing others. The ascended masters have taught us the rules, we just weren't listening. We have to become like God. God is pure, innocent, perfect, unlimited, merciful, loving, and joyful. If we are not these things, then we will experience the opposite until we become these things."

"Then why do we have evil? What's the point? Why do we need evil to become these things?" she asked.

"To know love, you have to experience hate. To know mercy, you have to experience cruelty. To know joy, you have to experience pain. And on it goes," Johnny replied. "Without these, the test would not be complete. There must be the full gamut of experience. The extremes of both good and evil. Without these, experiences are limited. If there is one thing the Creator avoids, it is setting limits on what is possible. Ultimately, the Creator wants to experience everything.

"Understand that we are God, we are the Creator, so when we expose ourselves to these experiences, so does the Creator. These are shared experiences that benefit everyone. You might think that an act of evil has no benefit, but that's not true. All experiences ultimately benefit the Creator. How an act of evil manifests is much more complex than is understood, and is not as simple as one person going astray. The bottom line is this. Life is perfection. Life cannot go astray. No one can make a mistake. Why? Because we are the Creator, and the Creator only knows perfection. Let me be clear. This plane of existence is an illusion. What is experienced here is not real. It is only a school. If you want an analogy, consider this plane of existence a computer game that you are playing. Those images on the screen of the computer game are not real."

The reporter hesitated. "What you are describing is similar to the movie The Matrix, and we are living in a simulation."

Johnny nodded. "Sure, it's not a bad analogy."

The reporter was still skeptical. "I understand your argument that we come here to evolve the soul, but I don't understand why we have to expose ourselves to so much cruelty. Why does God force people to endure so much hardship?"

"No one incarnates on this planet without it being their free choice. We gladly come here for the opportunity to expose ourselves to these tests and experiences. In fact, we are extremely grateful for the opportunity. There are many souls who do not get to come. There are billions more souls who want to come than there are bodies on this planet. To say we are lucky to be here is a vast understatement. If you only knew how lucky you are to be here at this time, you would be on your knees, weeping with gratitude."

"Why would the gratitude be so intense?" she asked.

"Because of the meaning of life. This planet and civilization offers the ability to expand the soul at a rapid rate. When you come here, you are almost guaranteed soul growth. And any form of growth is more precious than you can imagine. To achieve the level of an ascended master is almost beyond comprehension, yet every soul has this potential, and so much more, once it is achieved."

The reporter looked into Johnny's eyes. "That's enough for today, but I want you to come into the studio for some follow-up questions. Can you do that?"

Johnny smiled. "Sure, no problem."

Chapter One : Near-Death Experience

The reporter and the cameramen laughed at his confidence. But they both knew they had a big story.

※ ※ ※ ※ ※

The next day, the interview played on the local *CNBS* station, and then the San Francisco newspapers picked up the story and came and did an interview. It wasn't long before Johnny's blog was a popular website.

When Johnny went to school, he was ostracized by some of the students. This is typical human behavior. What you don't understand, you attack. His friends were more understanding and continued to hang out with him, although none of them read his blog or watched his YouTube videos.

Johnny did not talk about spirituality with his friends, although it was difficult at first to keep his mouth shut. He knew from the knowledge he had learned to only share it with those who were interested. It turned out that only souls with a propensity for understanding spirituality were interested in the meaning of life. Every soul was at a specific level of spiritual awareness, and this level determined their ability to grasp spiritual concepts.

Johnny learned two important rules from his download of knowledge. First, do not try to explain spiritual concepts to those who are not ready. From this rule, he knew that there is no reason to try to save anyone or explain to an atheist that they are wrong. Second, do not try to understand evil. Leave it alone, and it will leave you alone. The best way to combat darkness was to shine your own inner light. If you shine your light by using a frequency of love, then darkness will leave you alone. It is only when you give darkness attention that it gains a foothold.

From following these two rules, Johnny's life was pretty simple. He did his morning hand prayer and then tried to maintain the ideals in the prayer all day: serving the soul instead of the ego;

being grateful instead of prideful; maintaining integrity and virtue; staying connected to his heart-center for guidance; accepting everything that happened in his life with gratitude; and, remaining humble and neutral, with a bias of unconditional love. He tried to always remain positive with a frequency of love because he knew that was humanity's destiny, and he wanted to be an example. He did not discuss spirituality with those who were not ready for it, except on rare occasions when he felt impelled to speak, such as when he did interviews. He also avoided the temptations of life and remained virtuous.

What Johnny was doing was nothing special. It was how all advanced souls lived. He was doing it for several reasons. First, it made sense to him after what he had learned. Second, he wanted to prepare for what he knew was coming. Third, he knew it was the best way to expand his soul's awareness. It was the path of the ascended master.

He had the opportunity to enjoy the temptations of the world, and all that the material world had to offer. But that was not going to get him what his soul needed. He knew deep inside that his soul had another agenda. His soul had a strong desire to evolve, and perhaps ascend during this lifetime. He knew that it has been done before by some ascended masters, and that with the planet ascending, some people would as well.

He had no desire to raise a family, or go to college and have a profession. His passion for spirituality overrode these desires. He had no desire to achieve something to be happy. His motives were much different than the average person. Others had less focused passion, but it generally revolved around an elusive desire to be happy. These desires around happiness were usually filled through emotional relationships, financial rewards, material abundance, or ego satisfaction. None of these were what Johnny was interested in obtaining. He wanted something more, something that he could literally take with him when his soul left his body.

Chapter One : Near-Death Experience

Johnny knew that this world was an illusion. What happened in this world had only one purpose, which was spiritual growth. Everything else was a charade. The anger and fear that people felt was created for the purpose of growth. It was no more real than their temporary bodies. It was no more real than a staged play at the theatre.

What made recognizing the illusion so difficult is that life feels so real on this planet. People cannot grasp the perfection of life, or that separation is an illusion. When they see cruelty and unfairness and all of the depravity that exists on this planet, they cannot see the perfection. Ironically, seeing the perfection is the first step to knowing God. It is when you see the perfection that you become compassionate and can finally hold unconditional love in your heart. Not just for those you love, but for all of humanity.

The hardest part of the spiritual journey is grasping that there are no good guys or bad guys. Instead, all is God. It is one. And the God who we recognize as the Creator can only exist as perfection. God only knows unconditional love and complete compassion. That is the Creator. That is our core. That is who we truly are.

When you go looking for God, you will find that the only path with a high success rate is the one Johnny outlined in the hand prayer. While there are many different ways to achieve that path, they are all essentially the same. You have to become pure in your heart and live that purity. And from that purity, love will manifest in everything you do.

The path of the ascended master is one of love. Achieving that focal point of love is not easy to obtain, but it was something that Johnny was going to try to do. It was his mission in life, and he was going to help as many people as possible who had this same mission.

Until recently, attempting to follow the path of the ascended master was a futile undertaking for but a tiny minority of people. However, the energy on the planet had been changing since the late 1980s. Now, the energy was becoming conducive for many to undertake this spiritual path. Not only was Johnny excited about following this path, but he was also excited about helping others to do it as well.

Chapter Two

THE MEETUP GROUP

After the *CNBS* story aired in San Francisco, the local newspapers came and interviewed Johnny and ran stories of their own. It wasn't long before everyone at Johnny's school knew who he was. An amazing thing happened, many of the students started reading his blog and sending him emails. He decided to create a meetup group of aspiring teenage ascended masters.

One of the students at his school had a large game room in his backyard. His dad had built it as a man cave to watch sports and smoke cigars. It was a perfect place for twenty people to meet once a month.

At the first meeting, sixteen people showed up. It was decided that they would only have twenty members because that was all the room could hold comfortably. Those who showed up at the first meeting knew that they had just joined a very exclusive and important group. They would be friends for years to come.

Johnny was the leader, even though he was one of the youngest. Nearly all of the kids were from his high school, although a few were from the surrounding area. Any teenager in the surrounding area was eligible to join.

After everyone was seated, Johnny began the meeting.

"Welcome, everyone. Thanks for coming. I don't know about you, but this is very exciting. We get to help each other become ascended masters. This is going to be fun, but it's also serious business. As you will find out, this is my passion. I'm all in, and I hope that you will be too.

"The path of an ascended master is not easy, and I'm sure some in this room are going to fail. We should put a couple of rules in place to maintain the integrity and purity of our group. First, no one should come to the meetings high on alcohol or drugs. Second, no one should become a disruption to what we are trying to accomplish."

"How are we going to define disrupting?" someone asked.

"I have an idea," one of the girls said. "We can vote people out like they do on those real-life television shows."

Everyone nodded.

"Okay, that's fine," Johnny said. "If anyone feels that someone is disrupting the meetings, they can tell me. After I get a few complaints, I will put it up for a vote. If two-thirds vote for banishment, then so be it."

Johnny scanned the room. "How does that sound?"

Everyone nodded, so Johnny continued. "Okay, then. Those are the only two rules. Don't show up high, and don't disrupt the meetings."

"If someone brings food and I eat it all, is that disrupting?" one of the boys asked.

Several people laughed.

"No, that's just being rude," one of the girls said.

"What are we going to talk about tonight?" someone asked.

"I have a topic," another announced.

"Go ahead," Johnny said.

"The ego," he replied. "I watched your interview on *CNBS*, and you said that we either serve the ego or the soul. How do we serve the ego?"

Johnny was quick to answer. "Until you marginalize the ego, that's all you do. The ego is literally in charge of your life until you turn it off. I'll bring Eckhart Tolle's book next month, and you can pass it around. Understanding the ego is perhaps the most important lesson to becoming an ascended master. The ego stands for 'edging God out.' That is what the ego does. It blocks your

Chapter Two : The Meetup Group

soul and takes control of your life. Our job is to marginalize the ego and let the soul be in control. I call this marginalizing the ego.

"Tolle says this is accomplished through stillness in the present moment, and he is right. We have to meditate constantly, with a quiet mind, to control the ego. This allows us to create stillness and remain in the present moment. This stillness creates a gateway to the soul. You can also call this gateway our heart-center. And once you open it, you literally have access to guidance and truth from the soul. This guidance does not come from the brain, but the soul."

"Where does the soul reside?" a girl asked.

Johnny smiled. "I love that question. I wish more people asked it. The soul resides in the same place for everyone. The soul resides in the Creator's consciousness. Thus, our soul is literally connected to the Creator. No one in this room is self-contained. The source of your consciousness is not here. If you could follow it back to its source, you would find that it is the same source for everyone."

"Wow!" one of the girls said.

Johnny grinned. "Yes, wow. We are literally all from the same place. It is the ego's job to hide that knowledge from us, and it is powerful and masterful at achieving that goal. Today, every time you use your brain to make a decision, the ego is in charge. The only time the soul is in charge is when you quiet the mind and listen to the heart. Some would call this impossible, but I submit that it is the path to enlightenment."

"Every time the brain makes a decision, the ego is in charge...." a girl slowly repeated.

Johnny nodded. "Exactly."

"And you're saying that the ego is leading us astray from God?" the same girl asked.

Johnny nodded again. "Yes."

"That means that life itself, since everyone is constantly using their brains, is leading people astray," she said.

Ascension Training

Johnny nodded again. "Yes, life is a big charade where very few know the truth. The ego is hiding God, and also hiding the truth about life. People are living their lives in ignorance of the truth. Most people are living the opposite of how they would live if they knew the truth. However, they are learning lessons that are beneficial to the soul. In other words, there is nothing wrong with not knowing the truth while learning in a state of ignorance. What is the saying, 'Ignorance is bliss?'"

"So, you are implying that what the ego is doing is not a bad thing? That leading people astray, which often leads to awful experiences, is not a bad thing?"

"In fact," Johnny replied, "what the ego is doing is a good thing. It is allowing people to grow spiritually, even if they don't know it."

"Okay, my head's spinning now," someone said.

"I think I just had an epiphany," a girl said. "You are implying that the ego has a role to play to teach us lessons. But at some point, the soul exposes the ego for what it is, a false god."

Johnny pointed at the girl. "Exactly!"

"Is anyone recording this meeting?" someone asked.

"Yes, I am," a boy said.

The questioner nodded. "Okay, we need to keep these recordings, so that we can listen to them again. We should put them on the cloud, where we all have access."

"I'll upload them and send everyone the cloud account and password," the boy said.

"Are you volunteering to record them each month?" Johnny asked.

The boy nodded. "Sure. If I miss a day, I'll have Andy do it." He looked to his left, where Andy was sitting.

"Stop talking about geek stuff!" a girl said loudly. "This was getting really interesting."

Chapter Two : The Meetup Group

Several people laughed.

"Where were we?" Johnny asked.

"You said that the soul eventually exposed itself," a girl said.

"Yes, the ego will do everything it can to remain in charge and keep us mesmerized that the world is real, and everything and everyone is separate. But if you are an evolved soul, at some point, you will recognize that something is amiss. The ego will use materialism, sports, entertainment, food, shopping, sex, drugs, music, hobbies, you name it. It will use whatever temptation you are susceptible toward, to screw up your life. It knows your weaknesses. This is what makes it so powerful and such a worthy adversary. It knows which buttons to push to stay in control."

"I think I understand," a girl said. "The ego uses these desires to keep us mesmerized, but advanced souls begin to recognize that these desires are not the true path. They begin to recognize that something is missing, and then they go looking for it."

Johnny nodded. "They go looking for God."

"But sex, drugs, and rock and roll are fun. Can't I have fun?" one of the boys asked.

"To each his own," Johnny replied. "There is no correct path for finding God, and all roads eventually lead to enlightenment. Having fun is a choice. However, at some point, you will become more serious about finding God. At that point, sex, drugs, and rock and roll will lose their allure. Until they have lost that allure, have as much fun as you can. Get it out of your system."

"Are you condoning drugs, Johnny?" someone asked.

"I do not condone nor condemn. Like I said earlier, to each his own."

"Is that what you were downloaded?"

Johnny nodded. "Yes, all is perfection, and it is not for us to judge. It's funny, that's in the Bible, but no one believes it."

"Everyone thinks that God is going to judge everyone and decide their fate," a boy said.

"In many respects, they are right about the judgment of God," Johnny said. "But they don't understand how it works. There is no condemnation from God. Instead, there is absolute, unbiased appraisal. And most of this appraisal is done by ourselves. Our level of spiritual awareness dictates the outcome of our progression. We progress as we evolve. It is as simple as that."

"That's why we are on this planet, isn't it?" a girl asked. "We are here for only one purpose, the progression of our soul."

Johnny nodded. "For most people, that's true. In fact, it's true for nearly everyone on the planet. However, there are currently a lot of volunteers who came to help the planet awaken and create a more spiritually evolved civilization. These advanced souls are here for the event and not necessarily the progression of their soul."

Johnny paused and waited for a reply.

"So, we can't become an ascended master until we give ourselves a passing grade? We have to first do a personal appraisal and then ask God if He agrees?"

Johnny laughed. "That's pretty close, but not quite right. Our level of spiritual awareness is not a secret on the other side. There are no secrets in the higher spiritual dimensions, and all knowledge is available to everyone. When a soul has obtained the level of spiritual awareness required to be an ascended master, it is immediately known by everyone."

"Oh, my God!" a girl said incredulously. "Are you saying that every soul has a soul awareness level? We each have an awareness level that can be measured?"

Johnny sighed. "Sorry, but yes, it's true. We each have a level of spiritual awareness, and this level is known by all. Not only that, but we each have a personal history that is shared among everyone, as well. And this history is not the Cliff Notes version, but all of our experiences, which are stored in the Akashic Records."

Chapter Two : The Meetup Group

"Ugh," she replied. "I wish I didn't have a number. It makes it so competitive."

"At least you're eternal," another girl replied.

Some of them laughed.

"She's probably ahead of all of us," a boy said.

"Yeah, she's probably already an ascended master," another boy said.

They all laughed.

"When you say, 'To each his own,' are you implying that God condones sin?" a girl asked.

Johnny hesitated. "Your question implies that the answer is either yes or no, but that is not how God thinks. God allows free will and then accepts our choices with complete compassion and unconditional love. How we each choose to achieve enlightenment is our own choice. That path invariably will include something that you consider to be a sin. Which means that we have all been sinners. And to set the record straight, God is us, and we are God. So, do you think it's possible for God to sin?"

Johnny slowly shook his head from side to side. "Nope."

"Oh, my God!" a girl exclaimed. "Now I see why it's so hard to be an ascended master. This means that not only can we not judge others, but we have to love them, too!"

Johnny smiled. "It's easy once you begin to recognize that you are staring at yourself."

There was silence as Johnny waited for someone to reply.

"I get it," a boy replied. "You are saying that once we achieve a higher level of spiritual awareness, we will know that all is one. At that time, judgment will no longer have any meaning."

More silence.

"You're saying that we will literally begin to love everyone because we see them as ourselves?" a girl asked.

Johnny nodded.

"Wow, that's trippy," a girl said. "I hate nearly everybody. That kinda rocks my world."

A few people laughed.

"The core of who we are is love," Johnny said. "That's really the only thing that is real in this world. It's who we are, our true self. Everything else is an illusion. That's what gives us our eternalness. When God created us, He manifested us as a piece of love, which is basically what God is. This is why, when a mother looks at her baby for the first time, all she can think of is how much love she feels for the child. The core of her being is being touched."

"I thought God created us as a piece of light?" a boy asked.

"Yes, that's true," Johnny replied. "Our soul is pure energy which radiates as light. This energy is indestructible. Only the Creator can put out our light."

"Does that ever happen?" a girl asked.

"Yes," Johnny replied, "but let's save that for another time. You can only process so much in one night. I'll let you ponder the answer for next time."

Johnny looked at the clock on his phone. "Our time is up, although anyone can hang out for another hour if they want. Steve told his father it's for two hours. I scheduled the meetup for one hour to give us time to hang out. And one hour of speaking is about all I can handle. Also, I'm addicted to the Internet, and I like to be online at night."

Everyone laughed.

"Speaking of the Internet. On my website, there is a reading list of ten books. Try to read at least one book per month. Consider it required reading if you want to become an ascended master."

A few people groaned.

Johnny made his way to the door, and a girl stopped him. "Do you need a ride? I know you're only fourteen."

Johnny smiled. "I have a bike."

Chapter Two : The Meetup Group

"That's another reason you scheduled it for one hour," she said. "You want to get home before it's dark."

Johnny smiled. "You have me figured out. What's your name?"

"Julie. I can give you a ride when the days get shorter."

"I would like that," Johnny said.

Julie was a junior and sixteen. She had short red hair and was petite and attractive. Johnny looked into her blue eyes and couldn't wait until October.

* * * * *

The next day at school, Johnny saw Julie and walked over to say hello.

"Did you like the meetup group last night?" he asked.

"I downloaded Tolle's book and read half of it last night. It's awesome."

Johnny smiled. "Why don't you come over tonight, and we can talk about it?"

Julie smiled. "I like your style. What time?"

"After dinner. Seven or eight." Johnny reached into his pocket. "Here's my card. It has my phone number on it. Call me, and I'll text you my address. I live on Henderson near the college."

Julie took the card and looked at it. "What's with the card?"

"I do public speaking, and people ask for my contact information. My dad said it was a good idea to carry them."

"Cool. I'll see you tonight." She smiled at him as she walked away.

Ascension Training

✳ ✳ ✳ ✳ ✳

When Johnny's dad opened the door for Julie, he was impressed. Even if he didn't understand Johnny's spirituality, it seemed to be helping Johnny's personal life.

"Johnny is in his room. He seems to live on his computer. It's upstairs on the left. The door will be closed, and you will hear loud music. Just knock. He is expecting you."

Johnny's dad grinned.

Julie climbed the stairs, her iPad with Tolle's downloaded book in her hand.

She knocked on Johnny's door, and he opened it with a smile. "Come on in."

He closed the door behind her and turned down the music.

"Your dad seems nice."

"He's okay, but we don't talk much. He likes to watch TV and play golf, two things I'm not interested in."

"Where is your mom and sister?"

"How do you know about them?" Johnny asked.

"The newspaper article."

"Oh yeah. They are out. I think they went shopping. My sister will probably knock on my door when they get home. She doesn't know about privacy."

Julie laughed.

"I brought the book."

"We can talk about it," Johnny said.

Julie smiled. "You don't care about the book, do you? You just wanted me to come over."

"Is it that obvious?" Johnny laughed.

"It's okay. I get asked out a lot. Boys like cute girls."

Johnny smiled. "Can you blame us?"

"No kissing on the first date," Julie said.

Chapter Two : The Meetup Group

"I wasn't planning to kiss you. And we can talk about the book."

"Actually, I would rather talk about your near-death experience. I just brought the book because I mentioned it today."

"What do you want to know?" Johnny asked, lying on his bed, leaning back against a pillow.

"Where should I sit?" Julie asked.

Johnny laughed. "Sorry, there aren't a lot of choices. On the bed, I guess."

Julie sat on the bed and crossed her legs, Indian style. "This is fine."

Johnny waited for her to ask a question.

"Tell me about the experience," she said.

"Okay. I saw the car coming out of the corner of my eye. I never saw it clearly. When I was turning my head to see it coming, that's when it hit me. I felt the pain of the impact, and I felt my body flying through the air, but once I hit the ground, my soul left my body, and I was in another dimension. I could tell nobody could see me because it was a different realm."

"What do you mean?" she asked.

"The car that hit me had stopped, and the people had gotten out and were trying to help me. But I was dead, lying on the ground. There was nothing they could do for me. I was watching from the other side, as a spirit, as a soul, as a light being. My memories were all intact. It was me, but I had become a spirit. I was trying to understand how I was thinking without a brain when a light being showed up."

"What did they look like?" she asked.

"Wispy light. Kind of like a ghost, but more defined. Not human, but otherworldly looking. It's very hard to describe because we don't have anything to compare it to. But he did look like an elderly man to a certain extent."

"And he took you away?" she asked.

Johnny nodded. "Yep, he telepathically said, follow me, and we were gone. Faster than Superman."

She laughed. "What did it feel like being this spirit?"

"I felt bliss. I felt like I was home. The feeling of love was so intense, it was almost hard to bear at first. Then I recognized that this feeling of love was natural and normal. I wanted to stay there. It was so wonderful."

"What was your body like?" Julie asked intrigued.

"It was my soul. It was pure energy. You could see through me. I was translucent. I didn't have a mirror, so I didn't see my face, but I think I had similar facial features."

"What did everything look like?"

Julie's eyes widened in anticipation of the answer.

"Amazing doesn't begin to describe it, and paradise is not a big enough word to explain what I saw. It was like science fiction and animation combined. Everything was made of energy, yet it could be manipulated with your mind. In some respects, it didn't look real. Yet, I knew that it was more real than where we live today.

"There were crystal buildings of all different colors. There were green rolling hills, with waterfalls and rainbows. Colorful birds flying around. Horses and tigers walking side by side in peace. There was no need for food. Everyone and everything was self-energized by their connection to source. There was no individuality. Everyone was connected and literally one consciousness. In fact, we could communicate with each other simply by thinking. It was all telepathic."

"How long were you there? I read that you were dead for ten minutes?"

"There is no time there, so I don't know. But it wasn't very long. It was a short talk, and I was back in my body. Once we arrived, I was in this crystal building standing before this highly evolved being."

Chapter Two : The Meetup Group

"What did he look like?"

Johnny laughed. "Everyone asks me that. People want to know what we look like when we die. He could have appeared any way that he wanted. The soul can manifest any form that it wants. This advanced being appeared to me as I would expect a wise old soul to look. He was old with white hair and a wrinkled face, and he wore a white robe with a gold belt. He was translucent like me, and I could see through him if I looked hard enough. He looked real enough, but I knew that he was a manifestation. The soul is much more intelligent in the spiritual dimensions. When I asked my mind what I was seeing, my soul received an information packet that described him in detail."

"A what?" Julie asked, with a perplexed look.

"An information packet. When we communicate telepathically, we get information sent to us in dense information packets. These contain much more information than a sentence or two. In fact, they can be entire books or several books."

"So, your soul received an information packet that told you all about this being?"

Johnny nodded. "Yeah."

"But where did it come from?" Julie asked, with the same perplexed expression.

"It's so amazing in the spiritual dimension. All information is known and retrievable. Whatever you want to know, you simply ask, and it arrives in your mind. It seems like everyone shares the same mind, which is infinite and all-knowing."

"That's too weird."

Johnny laughed. "Trust me, it felt natural. And it's really cool."

"Then, there are no secrets, once you are in heaven."

"Nope," Johnny replied.

"Okay, what did he tell you?"

"The first thing he said was that I have to go back. That's not what I wanted to hear, because I wanted to stay. That place is home. Then he asked me if I wanted the answers to the questions I keep asking. But he said the answers would come at a price, and did I want the burden?

"I told him I would do anything to have the answers. That no burden could be too much. Then he told me he would give me the gift of knowledge if I agreed to share it with humanity. I told him, yes, that I would, and he began sending me packets of information. Then he smiled and left."

"What happened next?" she asked.

I looked around at the birds flying, and then I was back in my body. It was not a pleasant re-entry. One moment I was a powerful, all-knowing soul, and the next, I was back in my body, hurting really bad."

"Do you feel like a different person now, after you came back?"

Johnny nodded. "Oh yeah. I'm not the same Johnny who died in that street for ten minutes. I know too much to go back to being that naive kid. No longer do I live by faith. Now, I live by knowing. I know that I'm an eternal soul. I know that I'm here to expand my soul awareness. And I also know that I am here to help the planet ascend. That was part of my download. I now know why I am here, and I've had a glimpse of the future."

"Wow, that's intense," Julie said incredulously.

"And I can help you to find your soul so that you also live by knowing. I know how to teach you."

Julie smiled. "Very cool. Are you going to show the meetup group?"

Johnny nodded. "Yeah, that's why I started it."

"And you want us to also help the planet ascend?"

Johnny smiled. "You got me figured out."

Chapter Two : The Meetup Group

Julie squinted her eyes. "The planet ascending sounds almost too fantastic to believe."

Johnny hesitated, contemplating what to say. "Planetary ascension is what the planet is currently doing. It is evolving into a higher energy frequency to support unity consciousness, as well as portals into the fourth and fifth dimensions."

"What? How am I supposed to understand that?" Julie started at him with an open mouth of disbelief.

Johnny laughed. "Don't worry, I'll explain it."

"Let's save it for next time. I need to get home before I'm late."

Julie got up to leave and grabbed her iPad off the bed.

"Do you kiss on the second date?" Johnny asked.

Julie smiled. "I haven't decided yet if you're too young. We might have to wait until next year."

"I'm almost a sophomore. There's only two months left in the school year."

Julie laughed as she got up to leave. "Good try."

"Thanks for coming over."

Julie turned and smiled as she walked out the door.

Chapter Three

PLANETARY ASCENSION

"Who was that girl that came over last night?" Johnny's mother asked.

Johnny and his family were seated around the dining room table eating dinner. All eyes were on Johnny, waiting for him to answer.

"Her name is Julie. I met her at my monthly meetup group."

"Dad said that she's older than you," his sister said.

"Yes, she's sixteen. So what?" Johnny said defensively.

"Johnny's got a girlfriend," his sister teasingly sang.

"I don't know about that," his dad said while passing the potatoes.

"Why?" his sister asked. "Is she pretty?"

"Okay, everyone stop," Johnny said impatiently. "She's not my girlfriend."

* * * * *

At the next meetup group, Johnny decided to talk about ascension. From his perspective, it was the most important topic and the reason he was on the planet. He wasn't sure how many of the members of his meetup group were ready to take it seriously, but he had to find out.

"Hello, everyone. Tonight, we have four more members, and we are officially a full group. However, after tonight I would not be surprised if we have a few openings. I'm going to talk about ascension, and for some of you, it's going to sound strange. Most of you have probably read some of my comments about ascension on my blog, but tonight, I am going to ask you to begin preparing for it.

"We are aspiring ascended masters, and ascension is what we are striving to achieve. If we can ascend in this lifetime, we will become ascended masters. However, this process is extremely difficult, because we have to obtain mastery over our thoughts and emotions. We have to discipline our minds to control our thoughts and live with integrity, gratitude, and virtue. This will allow us to open our heart-center and live with a frequency of love. The heart-center gives us access to our soul, also called our higher self or true self. This opens a channel to guidance that we can trust."

Johnny scanned the group and continued in his serious tone.

"The key to opening this channel is love, because love is the foundation of the soul. In actuality, love is what we are really learning. We are learning how to love each other, how to love ourselves, and how to love God. All of our lessons on this planet are related to love. So, that needs to become our focus.

"Constantly say out loud the things you love about your life and the things you love to do. This will create a love energy around those things. Our beliefs and intent are reflected back to us. We are God, and the universe gives us what we want and what we ask for.

"Ironically, we are re-learning love. When we are born, we come in with perfect innocence and integrity. For most of us, in the first couple of years, all we know is love. This closeness to love creates a very clear channel to our soul. For this reason, many children remember their past lives. Their memories don't come from their brain, but from their open channel to their soul. These are soul memories.

"Isn't it interesting that the Bible says in Matthew 18:3, 'Unless you are converted and become like children, you will not enter the kingdom of Heaven.' Thus, we need to re-find our innocence. The Bible was absolutely correct, and that is what we shall do. And isn't it interesting, that those who stray the most from love

Chapter Three : Planetary Ascension

and the most from innocence, have the most difficult lives? And those who love the most and have an abundance of love in their lives, are the most satisfied and fulfilled? Love clearly is the way.

"So, to become an ascended master, we have to become ingrained in love. In fact, love has to be the focal point of our minds. It is what we have to think about at all times because that is what the soul thinks about."

"How do we do that?" someone asked.

"I'll teach you, but first, everyone needs to understand why we are going to do it. I need to explain what ascension is all about."

Everyone was listening intently, so Johnny continued.

"Each of us vibrates at a certain frequency, a certain tone. This frequency is what creates our level of spiritual awareness. It is our soul frequency, and it is the totality of our past thoughts, beliefs, actions, and behaviors. It is who we are, and we are each in control of this frequency. We can change it and make it better. The higher our frequency, the more aware we become. An ascended master vibrates at an extremely high frequency, which allows them to travel inter-dimensionally."

Johnny paused and scanned a few faces, which looked surprised.

"The planet itself also vibrates at a certain frequency. The planet's frequency is comprised of the mass consciousness and is encompassed in what can be called the crystalline grid. This energy grid is what allows the mass consciousness on the planet to interact. Thus, our lives are severely impacted by this mass consciousness. On a subconscious level, we can feel all that is occurring everywhere in the world...."

"You mean, we are all connected to this mass consciousness?" someone interrupted.

Johnny nodded. "Yes, everything and everyone is connected, and the mass consciousness constantly impacts our lives. It includes thought forms that people give power to, which ripple across humanity."

"You mean our mass thoughts are creating the world as we know it?" someone asked.

Johnny nodded. "Yes, exactly. But here's where it gets interesting. The planet and its mass consciousness is currently raising its frequency. This started happening in the late eighteen hundreds, but really kicked into gear in the nineteen sixties."

"What happens when the frequency rises?" someone asked.

Johnny smiled. "Lots of good things, although it might get worse in the near term before it gets better. The planet has decided that the era of duality needs to end before the planet is destroyed by avarice, greed, violence, and indifference. Duality can only end by the elimination of time, which requires the planet to ascend to a higher dimension."

"Are you talking about the fourth and fifth dimensions?"

Johnny nodded. "Yes, and it is already happening. Portals between the third, fourth, and fifth dimensions are already opening up. These portals allow bleed-through between the dimensions. Thus, people are starting to experience these other dimensions, and this will continue and become more widespread."

"What do they experience?" someone asked.

"It starts with fourth-dimension changes. People begin to experience psychic abilities, such as telepathy, or they begin to hear voices in their head, whereby they are channeling discarnate beings on other dimensional planes of existence, or perhaps their spirit guides."

"This is strange," someone said.

"Yes, it is extremely strange," Johnny replied. "And if some of you get up and walk out, or do not return next month, I will understand."

Johnny paused and scanned the room to see if anyone was going to leave. There were no takers, so he continued.

Chapter Three : Planetary Ascension

"Some of you may begin to experience bleed-throughs of fifth-dimensional consciousness. You will recognize this if time begins to get wonky. The present moment will feel strange as if time is standing still. Past and future events will appear to be happening at the same time. These are actually tests by the soul to see if you are ready to experience these higher dimensions. If your reaction is fear, then the experiences may stop. However, if you allow the experience to intensify, then you can literally expand your consciousness."

"I've read that ascension is a process of letting go," someone said. "Are we letting go of our humanness and becoming a higher being?"

"Yes," Johnny replied, "but I would say, we are letting go of our individualness, and becoming our multi-dimensional self."

"I've read that ascension is about mastery of thoughts and emotions," someone said.

Johnny smiled. "Beautiful. I love the questions. That is exactly what ascension is about, because the only way to obtain the higher frequencies of the fourth and fifth dimensions is to be able to control your thoughts in a positive manner through the expression of love. You have to obtain spiritual integrity through self-mastery. Conversely, if you think negative thoughts, which will lead to negative emotions, they will manifest nearly instantly in the higher dimensions. The reason for this is that there is no time there. Time only exists in the third and fourth dimensions.

"This is where it gets incredibly interesting. As the planet achieves higher frequencies, the manifestation of thought increases. Thus, those with negative thoughts will literally undermine themselves. They will be their own worst enemy."

"Do you mean that violence and wars will be eliminated?" someone asked.

Johnny nodded. "Indeed. Peace on earth is coming. Eventually, only those who can hold spiritual integrity will be allowed to stay. I should add that this will take about four generations to be completed, but we get to be the first generation that puts it in motion. We are the progenitors."

"What is spiritual integrity?" someone asked.

"Basically, a pure heart, but it's also about loving yourself and loving others because of the objective truth that all is God and knowing that separation is a lie," Johnny replied.

"Now I get it!" Julie exclaimed. "The ego is doing everything it can to keep us from knowing the truth. And the soul waits with patience for us to learn that an open heart is the key to the kingdom."

"Me, too!" a boy exclaimed. "An ascended master in training is trying to obtain an open heart and live with spiritual integrity at all times."

Johnny smiled. "Yes, and there is a reason why is it important that we succeed at becoming ascended masters. Because we are here as volunteers to help the planet raise its frequency in order to ascend. By raising our frequencies, we raise the planet's frequency, and then we impact the mass consciousness, which leads to peace on earth and a new humanity based on love."

"In other words, we are here to help humanity," someone said.

"Oh, it is much bigger than that," Johnny replied. "Earth's ascension will impact the entire universe. It's a huge event, and we are right in the middle of it."

"We have a front row seat," someone said.

"Okay," Julie asked, "now that we know that the planet is raising its frequency and on a path toward ascension, how do we prepare for that?"

"First, by finding your soul, and I'll help all of you to do it," Johnny replied.

"Do we need to find our soul because that is the only way to raise our soul frequency?" someone asked.

Chapter Three : Planetary Ascension

Johnny pointed at the boy who asked the question. "Exactly. It is the gateway to spiritual awareness."

"I'm ready to find it," Julie said. "What are the steps?"

"You have to marginalize the ego and allow the soul to speak. You have to give the soul a voice, but this voice will speak through your heart and not your head. This will require that you create stillness in your mind. If you have a constantly chattering mind, then begin meditating. Without a quiet mind, the soul can't communicate. As Mary Magdalene wrote in her gospel, 'I go now to the silence.' It is the silence, in tandem with the intent of spiritual integrity that gives the soul a voice.

"The first step of achieving spiritual integrity is marginalizing the ego. You do this by doing my morning hand prayer each morning. The prayer is on my website. Start doing it every morning. Do not allow the ego to lead your life. Instead, begin to serve the soul by living in the present moment. Make the present moment your friend. Embrace uncertainty. Don't fear it. Accept everything that happens as perfection. Accept everything that happens as a blessing. At first, the ego will try to convince you that you should be upset when something goes wrong. But if you stay calm, with a quiet mind, trusting that all is well, the ego will lose its influence. This is the beginning of the soul taking over and guiding your life. Don't let the ego lead. Allow the soul to lead. You are going to have to learn how to do this.

"You do it by serving the soul. As you serve the soul, it will begin to make its presence known to you. It might take a month, it might take six months, or perhaps longer. But it will make its presence known if you marginalize the ego sufficiently and quiet the chatter in your mind. If you listen to the soul and not the ego, it is inevitable that the soul will make its presence known.

"Me and my soul and spirit guides have an ongoing conversation. I'm constantly amazed at how much they impact my life. I have to constantly thank them for their guidance. You will, too, once your relationship begins. And, I must reiterate, this is not fantasy. You will know that they exist.

"There are only two ways to live. One is to serve the ego, and the other is serving the soul. When you serve the soul, it will become your friend and make its presence known. Some of you may not yet have a high enough frequency to marginalize the ego. Your desires for selfish ends may be too strong. Each of you has the choice of choosing a lifestyle of temptations. The soul is not going to be highly accessible unless you commit to a lifestyle of spiritual integrity."

Johnny paused and waited for a reply, but there was just silence.

"Many of you are probably thinking, what do I have to give up? The most important thing to give up is your thoughts that are no longer congruent with spiritual integrity. No more judgment towards others. Now you allow people to choose their own path. No more selfish thoughts. Now you think in terms of humanity, and living for others. No more dwelling on the past or future. Now the focus is on the present moment.

"In addition to cleaning up your thoughts, you have to clean up your actions. If you follow the golden rule, that should be sufficient. Do unto others as you would like to be treated. Although, I would suggest avoiding avarice in all aspects of your life. Try to live simply."

"What about sex, drugs, and rock-n-roll?" someone asked.

"You don't have to abstain, unless you want to. These indulgences will not keep you from your soul. You can still pursue spiritual integrity and do anything in moderation. The key is who you are serving. If you are serving humanity and your soul, then it is acceptable. These are all part of life, and we came to live."

"When does our behavior cross the line and diminish our spiritual integrity?" someone asked.

"Oh, you will know. Your soul will tell you. In fact, the closer you get to your soul, the more the soul will dictate how you live.

Chapter Three : Planetary Ascension

The soul will be in charge. The soul can be just as powerful a taskmaster as the ego. However, you will find that you prefer the soul to the ego. The soul will give you guidance that leads down the narrow path to enlightenment."

"Isn't the soul the hidden gateway that we all seek?" someone asked.

"No, not everyone," Johnny replied. "It is the gateway for the true seeker. Until you are ready to find the gateway to enlightenment, it is not sought. In fact, most religions consider seekers to be heretics. Millions of people, mostly women, have been murdered by religions who have objected to people opening this gateway to the soul. Even today, newagers are considered odd, strange, and following beliefs that are deviant and unnatural."

"Will we be ostracized for being an ascended master in training?" someone asked.

Johnny laughed. "What do you think? Are you going to go home and tell your parents that the planet is ascending? How do you think that will go over?"

Everyone laughed, but there was a subtle tension in the room.

Johnny scanned the room. "We have to keep this to ourselves because no one will understand. We are the silent volunteers who are helping the planet. I do use my website to get out the message, but I don't recommend that you publicize your spiritual life. This is not something that very many people understand. And what people do not understand, they attack."

"But this is important!" Julie exclaimed. "The planet is changing, and people need to know about it. We shouldn't keep this a secret!"

Johnny looked at Julie. "I was told that I have to share the gift of my knowledge, but that doesn't mean that you have to. I don't recommend that you expose yourself to that ridicule. Keep it on the down low for now and wait and see if the world begins to change. At some point, the world is going to need our help. Wait until they ask."

"What help?" Julie asked.

Johnny hesitated. "Let's leave that for next time. We can talk about the future."

Julie groaned. "Does that mean you're finished for tonight?"

"Yeah, I have to fly to New York in the morning to film a documentary about NDEs. I need to get home to pack. Thanks, everyone, for coming. I'll see you next month."

Everyone stood up, and Johnny walked out the door first.

* * * * *

On the airplane, the passenger seated next to Johnny asked where he was going. He explained that he was going to New York to be in a documentary and told him about his near-death experience. The passenger was interested in metaphysics and asked Johnny if he had a glimpse of the future during his NDE.

Johnny nodded. "Yeah, but it's difficult to explain with words."

The passenger smiled. "My name is Roger. What is yours?"

Roger was in his thirties. He was wearing a suit in first class and looked like a successful businessman.

"I'm Johnny. Nice to meet you."

"Likewise. Now, why is it difficult to explain?"

"Well, we are transitioning into a civilization that is more focused in the fourth and fifth dimensions."

Roger raised his eyebrows. "And you know about the fifth dimension?"

Johnny nodded.

"I have a general understanding myself, but go ahead and describe it," Roger said.

"The fifth dimension is when time stops, but it's experienced while we are in our bodies. It's somewhat analogous to our imagination or dreams. It's where the past and future meld together,

Chapter Three : Planetary Ascension

and time no longer exists. It's a dimension where only the present moment exists. In many respects, it is where our soul awareness is brought down into our body...."

Roger interrupted. "So, are you saying it is basically our inner awareness?"

Johnny nodded. "Yeah, that's a good way to put it."

"Would you say that a psychic experience would be in the fourth dimension?"

"Yes," Johnny replied. "Any experience in the third dimension that could be described as esoteric would be a fourth dimensional experience."

"Is that where you had your NDE?" Roger asked.

"No, that would be in a higher dimension beyond the fourth. At least the fifth, but maybe even higher. What I experienced was probably beyond the fifth."

"What about meditation? Could those be fourth dimensional?"

"I suppose," Johnny replied. "It all depends on how deep the meditator goes to connect with the soul."

"How about telepathy? Is that fourth dimension?"

Johnny nodded. "As long as you remain in your body. If your spirit leaves your body, then it would be fifth."

"So, does that mean the soul can travel using the fifth dimension?" Roger asked.

Johnny smiled. "Yep. The fourth dimension is a gateway to the fifth. The fourth dimension begins to open up the true reality of the soul. The fifth dimension is experiencing that true reality. In the fifth dimension, there is neither time nor space. For instance, having an out-of-body experience is breaking through time and space. Today, many people are soul traveling inter-dimensionally, and this will become more common."

"You mean the fourth dimension is used as training to get to the fifth? Can you elaborate?" Roger asked, with intense interest.

43

Johnny laughed. "I'm glad we have a long flight. This might take some time."

Roger grinned.

"Millions of souls on the planet are currently using the fourth dimension to prepare for ascending to the fifth dimension. If they are successful in their preparation, they will be able to literally disappear from this reality and reappear in the fifth dimension."

Johnny paused to find out Roger's response.

"You mean that, once they are ready to live in the fifth dimension full-time, they will ascend to that level of reality?

Johnny smiled. "You are the first person that I have told that to. I've been afraid to explain it to anyone because it sounds so crazy. But trust me, it's true!"

Roger smiled. "I believe you. I've been reading about ascension for a couple of years. I just don't understand it very well."

"Don't worry," Johnny replied. "By the time we land, you will understand it perfectly."

"Continue," Roger said.

"To understand why we use the fourth dimension, you have to understand the fifth. It's very complex to explain, so we'll take it one step at a time. In the fifth dimension, we exist as unity consciousness. In fact, we literally share one consciousness. Once you rise to the upper fifth dimension, this consciousness has a foundation of love. For this reason, we make all choices from a selfless standpoint. Everything we do, everything we think, is done for the good of the whole. This eliminates conflict and disharmony. They don't exist. You could call this fifth-dimensional world and everything above it, Nirvana."

"What about the lower fifth dimension?" Roger asked.

"This is also called the lower astral planes, and they can be nasty and teeming with lesser evolved souls that do not have your best interests at heart. This is where demons and ghosts exist, and is not a place where you want to hang out."

"Is this hell?" Roger asked.

"It can be, if you want it to be. But it is not permanent. Nearly all souls eventually evolve."

Roger nodded.

"Now, because the world that we currently live in is completely different from the fifth dimension, in terms of how we think, the transition is very difficult. We have to use the fourth dimension to make this transition. This is done by getting closer and closer to the soul, and further and further away from the individualized ego. We have to literally leave our identity behind and merge with the unity consciousness. We have to become selfless."

"Keep going," Roger said, listening intently.

"The fourth dimension is the fifth dimension on training wheels. It gives us a glimpse of the true reality. We get to experience that reality, but only in tiny sips. The fourth dimension is literally the doorway or gateway to this ultimate experience. However, the ego identity knows that it can't go to the fifth dimension, and it will do everything it can to prevent us from going there. Because, once someone has experienced the upper fifth dimension, they won't want to come back."

"You are a perfect example of that fact," Roger interrupted. "After your NDE, you can't get the upper fifth dimension out of your mind."

"True, and I want more. Once you get a taste, you will want to experience it again. This is the natural state of things, and here's where it gets interesting. The planet itself is ascending. This is causing the crystalline grid to change and impact the way the third, fourth, and fifth dimensions interact. The planet is literally evolving its awareness, which is causing us to increase our awareness and vibrate at a faster rate, making the fourth and fifth dimensions accessible."

Roger put up his hand. "The fourth and fifth dimensions are becoming more accessible to people?"

Johnny nodded. "Yes, and it is increasing as each year goes by. In a few years, esoteric experiences will become common."

"This sounds like science fiction," Roger said. "You are implying that millions of people are going to begin a spiritual inner journey to find their soul. And that many of them are eventually going to literally disappear and ascend to the fifth dimension."

Johnny laughed. "It does sound crazy, when you put it like that."

"How would you put it?" Roger asked.

"We are experiencing a merging of the mind and the heart, which leads to a civilization that is more heart-centered. This inevitably leads to fourth dimensional experiences, which are precursors to spiritual evolvement."

"Okay, I get it," Roger said. "You are implying that this is a natural outcome."

"It is and it isn't," Johnny replied. "But whenever you find a dichotomy, you are closer to the truth. This merging of the mind and the heart is natural, but it took thousands and thousands of years to manifest. The timing is now, but it did not originate with this generation. In actuality, those who are here at this moment in time are very fortunate to be here. This is the 'it' place to be in the universe."

"I'm intrigued," Roger said. "Tell me more about this merging of the mind and heart?"

"Everything is an illusion in the world, and nothing is real, except one thing, the soul, which is comprised of love. At some point, this truth has to be exposed. And once it is, the path to spiritual awareness will come into vogue. That is when the merging begins."

"Do you know when?" Roger asked with a bit of trepidation.

Chapter Three : Planetary Ascension

"No, but it won't be long. It's going to happen soon. The truth is going come out."

"Do you know what will trigger it?" Roger asked with even more trepidation.

"Extraterrestrials are going land."

"Whoa! That might do it," Roger said, beginning to lose his cool composure.

Johnny smiled. "Don't you want to know what they are going to say?"

"Sure."

"Basically, three things. First, there is only one Creator, one God. Second, we are all connected to the Creator and share the same consciousness. Third, we are all God's in training through reincarnation."

Roger looked stunned. "That would change everything. Religions would wither away. War would stop. Society would reorganize."

Johnny nodded. "And the heart and mind would begin to merge."

"And the truth shall set you free," Roger said, very softly. "I always wondered what that meant. Now, I've got an idea what it means. As it is stated in the Bible, people thought it only applied to individuals. But the word 'you' can imply a civilization. Thus, the truth will set an entire civilization free."

"Well stated," Johnny replied.

"Okay, now that I know how and why it's going to happen, tell me more about the fifth dimension. That seems to be the key. It seems to be pulling us toward it."

"Exactly," Johnny said. "Good insight. The soul wants to evolve and become more and more like the Creator. The higher fifth dimension is a spiritual dimension where we exist as perfection, without any blemish. It is the ideal of Heaven. As I stated before, we no longer think in terms of self. Instead, we think in terms of unity. Our choices are made for the well-being of the whole. We share the same consciousness, so this becomes a very natural way to live.

"The fifth dimension does not have time, a future, or a past. Everything exists in the now moment. If you want to go somewhere, you think it, and you are there. This is possible because there is also no space. Everything exists as energy, which can be manifested into whatever you desire. There is no air, because we do not breathe. There is no disharmony, because there is only one consciousness, which is the manifestation of love."

"It sounds like Nirvana," Roger said.

"It is," Johnny replied.

"Then why are we here?"

"You can't just go to the higher fifth dimension. You have to evolve to that level first. Most people on this planet will not be going there anytime soon. It will take four generations before the majority can soul travel to the fifth dimension."

"Can you elaborate?" Roger asked.

"It's not an easy transition from the third to the fifth dimension. You have to turn inward and discover love of the soul. Currently, most people are serving their ego. They are making choices that serve themselves. Once you begin to serve the soul, you will begin to become selfless. This is the first step to shedding your individualness in order to ascend to the unity consciousness of the fifth."

"What happens if you fail to make this inner journey of finding the soul?"

"Very few souls fail," Johnny replied. "It just takes longer for some souls."

"But where do we go when we fail to ascend?" Roger asked, with a look of concern.

Chapter Three : Planetary Ascension

"You stay on the wheel."

Roger contemplated, then asked, "You mean we keep reincarnating until we eventually make it to the fifth?"

Johnny nodded. "Yes, eventually, nearly everyone makes it."

"Why is it so hard?" Roger asked.

"Because of the power of the soul. You wouldn't let a child play with the controls of a nuclear power plant. A soul must be evolved before it is ready to exist in an environment where it can manifest anything instantly."

Roger was quiet for the first time. He knew he was on the wheel, and he wasn't sure if he should try to get off.

"Can I get off the wheel in this lifetime?" he asked.

Johnny looked into Roger's eyes. "Maybe. Normally it would be nearly impossible, but because the planet is ascending, about twenty-five percent of the population has a chance to ascend with the planet. This is a once in an eon opportunity. I started an ascended master training group to help people ascend, but it's only for teenagers who live near me."

"Ascended master? I've heard that term. That is what you call discarnate beings who are highly evolved."

Johnny nodded.

"How come only twenty-five percent have the opportunity to ascend?"

"It depends on your level of soul awareness. And apparently, only twenty-five percent have a level high enough. I think you are in that group; otherwise, you wouldn't have listened to me. Your ego would have objected and told you that I was crazy."

Roger laughed.

"It's your soul that told you to listen to me," Johnny said.

"How would you define ascension?" Roger asked.

"It's a process of raising the vibration of the soul to a level high enough to ascend to the fifth dimension, although it can also apply to the planet."

"And how does one raise their vibration?" Roger asked.

"Souls are constantly raising their vibration through their reincarnation experiences. What you are asking is how does one make the final leap and achieve a level of vibration that allows ascending."

"Yes."

"This is achieved through the love of the soul and living a heart-centered existence. Once you love the soul enough, you will make choices that only support the soul's growth. The ego will be marginalized, and the soul will shine through. You will live an inspired life of high choices, setting an example for others to follow. Your choices will lead to your well-being, as well as society's well-being. You will spread love in everything that you do and live a life of selfless service, supporting the higher good."

"Ouch," Roger replied with a dejected look. "I don't think I can do that."

"If you are inspired, you can."

Roger laughed. "Yeah, if I had an NDE like you, then, yes, I probably could."

"Why not leverage my experience? All you need to do is believe it."

Roger contemplated. "Hmm. I'll consider it."

Chapter Four

JULIE'S HOUSE

While Johnny was in New York, he received a few texts from Julie, asking how it was going. He had a lot of free time on the set of the film and used some of it to text Julie. They ended up having long conversations. When he arrived home, she picked him up at the airport. Johnny had told his parents that he had a ride and not to pick him up.

When Johnny saw her in the baggage claim area, he wasn't sure if he should kiss her. He had been thinking about it the entire flight. Thankfully, Julie solved his dilemma by kissing him.

"That was nice," Johnny said.

Julie grinned. "I thought you would like it."

"You know, that's all I could think about on the flight."

"Boys are so one-minded. What's your bag look like?"

"It's bright blue with a yellow smiley face on it."

"Okay. So, how was your flight?" Julie asked, while looking for his bag.

"The lady next to me didn't say a word. It was quiet. I watched two movies."

"I bought a few books on ascension and started reading them," Julie said.

"Very cool," Johnny said excitedly. "We can talk about them."

"I think my parents would freak out if they saw them."

Johnny laughed. "Probably. My parents think I'm nuts. But what can they do?"

Julie shrugged. "Tell everybody, I guess."

"Does that bother you?"

"I don't know," Julie said, without emotion.

"Julie, we're going to be ostracized at first. It's inevitable. We're going to be labeled as freaks."

"But books are being written about it," Julie pleaded. "Many people take this seriously. It isn't science fiction."

Johnny looked into Julie's eyes. "To most people, it is considered science fiction. We are on the fringe, but that's how it has to be."

"God, I hate being an outcast when I am right," Julie said intensely.

"You don't have to talk like that," Johnny said. "As an ascended master in training, consciously choose words for the highest good."

Julie let out a deep breath. "Okay, I'll clean up my vocabulary, and focus more on the highest good."

Johnny pointed. "There's my bag."

Julie walked toward the bag and removed it from the baggage belt.

Johnny lifted the handle and began pulling it behind him as he walked. The bag rolled quietly on its wheels.

"It's not far," Julie said.

Once they arrived at Julie's new VW Beetle, Johnny placed the bag in the back. It was a beautiful day in San Francisco, and the drive was short to Walnut Creek. It would take thirty minutes without any traffic.

As they crossed the Bay Bridge from San Francisco to Oakland, Julie looked at Johnny. "Do you want to come over to my house, or will you get in trouble?"

Johnny smiled. "What trouble? My dad loves you."

Julie smiled. "What about your mom?"

"She doesn't know what to think of me. She's just praying I will outgrow my obsession with my NDE."

"You won't get grounded or anything?" Julie asked.

Chapter Four : Julie's House

"No, I've never been grounded. My parents aren't strict. They don't get mad."

"Cool. Stay for dinner."

Johnny smiled. "Sure. Let me text my dad and tell him I'll be home late."

"What if he says to come home now?" Julie asked.

"I'll ignore it."

Julie laughed. "Are you sure that is for the highest good?"

"Probably not, but adolescent love is a powerful thing. We can use it as an excuse."

Julie laughed. "We are a parent's nightmare. We're smarter than them, and we have no interest in listening to what they have to say."

"I'm not very rebellious. I do my homework and stay out of trouble. I don't go out much."

Julie laughed. "You do now."

Twenty minutes later, Julie pulled into her family's large half oval driveway. Her mother was an ophthalmologist, and her dad was an executive for a high tech company. They lived in a spacious, four thousand square foot house that was worth several million. Because her parents were very busy people, they did not eat family dinners most nights. Julie had a younger sister and they ordered out quite often. Their mother did not like to cook, and her parents tended to eat out most nights. The girls had the option of staying home, which is what they usually did.

Johnny left his suitcase in the car, and they walked into the house. It was Sunday afternoon, and her parents were casually reading and watching TV.

"This is Johnny," Julie said. "Johnny, these are my parents."

Johnny's mother rose to greet him. "I'm Jane. You can call me Dr. Davis, or Mrs. Davis. Or even Jane if you prefer." She smiled and shook his hand. She was very pretty, like Julie.

Johnny thought she was a very nice lady, and he liked her. "It's nice to meet you, Mrs. Davis."

"Hello, Johnny," Mr. Davis said, barely taking his eyes off what he was reading.

"Nice to meet you, Mr. Davis."

"Come on," Julie said. "Let's go upstairs."

When Johnny walked into Julie's room, he nearly gasped. "Wow! This is huge."

Julie smiled. "I'm a bit spoiled."

She had a king size bed, and the room was a large master bedroom.

"This is bigger than my parents' bedroom!" Johnny exclaimed.

"Come see my walk-in closet and private bathroom. It's really cool."

And she gave him a tour.

"This is decadent," he said. "We have a nice house, but you live like royalty. How big is that shower?"

"It's huge," she said. "I think the last owner was a professional athlete or someone famous. Wait until you see our movie room."

Johnny was silent.

"What?" she asked.

"Are you sure that you want to be an ascended master? You will have to live selflessly and with a simple lifestyle. That goes against everything about this room."

Julie laughed. "I could care less about my material things. Just because my parents are wealthy doesn't make me materialistic. And don't forget how successful your parents are, too. No one lives in Walnut Creek who doesn't have money."

"You're right," Johnny replied. "I was just checking."

"Now, let's talk about DNA!" Julie said excitedly.

She ran over and dived onto her bed.

"Did you know that our DNA is changing?" Julie asked.

Chapter Four : Julie's House

Johnny took off his shoes and found a place to sit on her bed.

"Yes, our DNA is starting to become dynamic and intelligent," Johnny said.

"This allows us to access the fourth and fifth dimensions."

Johnny nodded. "Our DNA is becoming more crystalline, which allows us to more easily interact with our multi-dimensional selves."

"I've already started," Julie said excitedly.

"What do you mean?" Johnny asked.

"I can travel outside my body. That's why I joined your meetup group."

"Why didn't you tell me this before?" Johnny asked.

"I'm telling you now."

"Okay, that's fine. When did you start doing it?"

"About a year ago, when I was fifteen. I've been reading metaphysical books since I was twelve. My aunt has them around her house in Santa Cruz. Last year, I read one about soul travel and started meditating to see if I could do it. I was surprised by how easy it was for me. My soul just pops out of my body."

Johnny smiled. "Where do you go?"

"Mostly just the lower astral planes. I'm afraid to go to the higher dimensions, but I know they're there."

"What are the astral planes like?" Johnny asked, intrigued.

"From what I read, it's different for everyone because your imagination plays a big part of what you see. It's very much like a dream world. It's translucent and other-worldly. When you first leave your body, it seems like you are a double of your body, which lies still in bed, although it is weightless and translucent. You can see your room, but it looks different. It's hard to explain. For instance, I can walk through the walls of my room, but it takes me to another level of reality, another dimension."

Johnny nodded. "So, if you leave this room, you leave this world?"

"Yeah. In many respects, it's like lucid dreaming, but it's much more real. Dreaming usually doesn't make sense, but out-of-body experiences are very realistic. I can literally travel to a beautiful place and hang out. It feels as real as this conversation."

"What you do there?"

"I usually like to fly around with the birds and then find a good view of a scenic valley with a meadow and a stream. There's a favorite place I visit. I go there and meditate."

"Do you see other people?"

Julie shook her head. "Very rarely, and if I do, I keep away from them. I read where it is best to keep to yourself. Some of the entities on the astral plane are actually living there. I am just a visitor."

"How can someone live there if you are only using your imagination?" Johnny asked, confused.

"Our imagination can overlap with other souls' imagination, and then we end up in the same reality."

Johnny contemplated. "So, your imagination can expand and integrate with other dimensions?"

Julie nodded. "The potential is unlimited. I have journeyed up a few levels and it gets more beautiful and wonderful, but I always turn around and come back. I'm not ready to go higher yet."

"Okay, tell me how you do it. How do you leave your body?"

"I use meditation. First, I quiet my mind and relax my body. Then, I begin feeling my soul energy body with my mind. Then I move my soul back and forth through my body. I consciously begin disconnecting my soul body from my physical body. Then it begins to tingle. Once it starts tingling, I breathe deeply through my nose and allow the tingling to increase into a vibration throughout my body. Once I feel the vibration get strong enough, I allow my soul to take me out of my body."

Chapter Four : Julie's House

"When do you know it's strong enough?" Johnny asked.

"The soul will let you know when it's ready to leave. You create the vibration with your intent and then allow the soul to take you somewhere."

"Do you float up?"

"I usually sit up, like I'm getting out of bed, but only the soul moves."

"Very cool," Johnny said. "And then what?"

"I fly to where my soul wants to take me."

"I'm going to have to try that," Johnny said in awe.

* * * * *

Johnny and Julie began dating and became nearly inseparable. She would pick him up in the morning, and they would go to school together. Then, after school was out, they would either go to her house or his. Because Julie's parents tended to be gone most of the time, they usually went to her house. Johnny became her mentor, and she became his muse.

As they drove home from school a couple of weeks later, Julie looked at Johnny. "What do you want to do?"

"I don't care," he replied. "Let's go hang out at your house."

"No, it's too nice today. Let's get ice cream and go to the park and talk about getting off the wheel."

Johnny looked at Julie. "Castle Rock?"

"Unless you want to drive up to Mount Diablo," Julie replied.

"No, Castle Rock sounds good. It's a shorter drive."

After buying some ice cream, they made their way to the park. Julie had done this a few times and came prepared with a blanket to place on the grass. They found a secluded place under the shade of a tree and sat down.

"When's the next meetup group?" Julie asked.

"Next week," Johnny said, while taking a spoonful of ice cream from his cup.

"Cool. I'm looking forward to it. I can't believe how much my life has changed since last month's meetup. It's all I think about."

"What about me?"

"Don't worry. You're my only boyfriend."

Johnny grinned. "I'm feeling puffy."

Julie laughed. "Be careful, you don't want to serve the ego."

"I can love you and not serve the ego."

"But isn't it a fine line?" Julie asked. "Isn't seeking pleasure the allure of the ego? Aren't we supposed to practice asceticism and live a simple life of virtue and innocence?"

"You've been doing your homework," Johnny replied.

"Just books you told me to read."

"Okay, I guess we have to get serious now," Johnny said, as he finished his ice cream. "To get off the wheel of karma, we have to raise our level of spiritual awareness to a very high level. This requires a stringent focus and discipline to live by the highest ideals. Conversely, a lifestyle of hedonism, narcissism, egotism, or materialism is counter to these ideals...."

Julie interrupted. "And these highest ideals include physical health and taking care of ourselves? Because by taking care of ourselves, we are helping humanity? Thus, we probably shouldn't be eating ice cream, since sugar is toxic to the body and dairy is generally not the healthiest food we can eat."

Johnny nodded. "In theory, yes, that is true. We should not consume unhealthy food. However, we are teenagers. A little bit of ice cream is not going to be that detrimental."

"And we don't have to be celibate or teetotalers?"

Johnny shook his head. "No, we don't have to join a monastery to become an ascended master. Although, many ascended masters in training will likely abstain from a large number of things that are considered questionable."

"Such as eating ice cream?"

"Yeah, a lot of ascended masters in training are vegan."

"Vegan? I don't know if I can give up meat," she said.

"It's not a requirement."

"Good, but what are the requirements?" she asked.

"You have to learn how to be heart-centered. Whereby the soul is the center of your universe, and is always leading you. The heart is the gateway to the soul, and you have to learn how to allow the soul to lead you."

Johnny waited for Julie to reply.

"I get that. The soul is the source of love, and that is what the highest good is all about. We have to constantly tap into that love and share it."

Johnny nodded. "Yep, that's what it's all about."

Julie put down her empty ice cream cup. "And to be an ascended master, we have to learn how to do this at all times?"

"Correct," Johnny replied. "We have to resonate love in everything we do. We have to accept everything that happens as perfect, as either a blessing or an opportunity. This requires that we become neutral and not react to events."

Julie's eyes lit up. "I think I understand. We have to allow love to literally flow in our lives. Our lives should exude a frequency of love."

Johnny nodded. "Yes, but it's not easy. The ego will play every trick it knows to shut this flow off. Because when love is truly flowing, the ego is completely marginalized."

"How can the ego shut off the flow?" Julie asked.

"By engaging the brain and pushing our buttons. Once the ego gets the brain thinking of mischief and temptations, the gateway to the soul, our heart-center, shuts down."

"So, no gateway, no love?"

"Correct," Johnny replied. "Love comes from the soul."

"That's why people say that love comes from the heart."

Johnny nodded. "Yep, society got some things right."

"So, if I understand what you said, the key is learning how to open up our hearts so that the soul can shine through. Conversely, we need to keep our minds quiet so that the mischief maker, the ego, can't disrupt this flow of love."

Johnny smiled. "You're a prodigy."

"Now I'm feeling puffy."

Johnny laughed.

"How do we open our hearts?" Julie asked.

"It's a process, and it's difficult. That's why I started the meetup group. I'm going to help you with the process. It takes a lot of work."

"That is what the morning hand prayer is all about?" Julie asked.

"Exactly. You have to train your mind to marginalize the ego, become neutral, and focus more on being heart-centered. No one can become heart-centered overnight. But we are all teenagers, and we have lots of time."

"And until we learn how to live being heart-centered, we are stuck on the wheel?"

Johnny nodded.

"Tell me more about the wheel," she asked.

"It's called a reincarnation cycle. Once you begin a cycle, you choose a role that you want to learn. For instance, I'm currently a priest-scholar. My main role is that of a priest, and my sub-role is a scholar. I was told this, but it fits me perfectly. A priest learns about spiritual matters. A scholar is a collector of knowledge. Thus, I'm a collector of spiritual knowledge.

"When you pick a role and begin a reincarnation cycle, you start at the beginning. At that initial point, you are an infant soul, and you have no understanding of God. Then you progress up

Chapter Four : Julie's House

the ladder to baby soul, young soul, mature soul, and finally, old soul. I'm currently a fifth-level old soul."

"At the end of this cycle, do you become an ascended master?" Julie asked.

"No, I wish it was that easy. You can't get off the wheel just by living a complete cycle. For this reason, you often have to pick another role and do another cycle."

"Oh my God! Lifetime after lifetime."

"Yes, thousands," Johnny said. "And to make it even more difficult, you usually can only become an ascended master during the old soul stage. That's normally the only time you are ready to make an attempt of being heart-centered. If you miss your opportunity, then you have to start over as an infant soul."

"So, becoming an ascended master and achieving spiritual freedom is a big deal?"

"It's huge. There are six billion souls on this planet, and normally, less than one percent would achieve spiritual freedom after a lifetime. But this lifetime, the chances are much greater. I would say about five percent have a good chance, and only because these souls are here for a reason. They came for the opportunity that exists today. There are a lot of advanced old souls on the planet at this time."

"What happens if you don't graduate and you are stuck on the wheel?"

"You go back to your spiritual group. This is the group of souls we are working together with to get off the wheel. Usually, this group reincarnates together and helps each other to make spiritual advancements. Many families on this planet are from the same soul group."

Julie got up. "This is getting depressing. I'm ready to go."

"Yeah, no one likes being stuck on the wheel," Johnny said, as he gathered up the blanket.

"I wish it was easier to get off," Julie said. "I almost feel like everyone here is a prisoner."

"Don't get stuck in negative thinking," Johnny said, as they walked through the park toward Julie's car. "It's very important to remain positive. The Creator, and our true self, only knows unlimitedness, wellness, success, aliveness, joy, et cetera. We need to align to that energy to be an ascended master."

Julie nodded. "I know that negative beliefs, negative thoughts pull us down."

"It's important that we remain in a state of grace, a state of gratitude," Johnny said.

Julie nodded. "I know that we are all here of our own choice and that we should be grateful for this opportunity. But it still feels like a prison, compared to what you experience in the fifth dimension."

"I've had those thoughts, too," Johnny said. "But I've come to the conclusion they are just ego traps. The ego is trying to convince us that God is cruel, and that simply isn't true."

Julie opened the car door and looked at Johnny. "I agree. It is a trap. After all, we are eternal souls and Gods in training. If we can't be grateful for that, then we have many more lessons to learn."

Johnny smiled as he got in the car.

Chapter Five

THE FUTURE

A week later, Johnny and Julie walked into the meetup room together. They were the last to arrive and knew instantly that something odd was happening. Everyone was huddled around and talking about something that seemed urgent. They didn't even notice Johnny and Julie's arrival.

"What's happening?" Julie said to the group in a concerned voice.

They stopped talking and turned to face Johnny and Julie.

"Steven had to sneak out of his house to come tonight. His parents think we are a cult group," someone said.

"My dad caught me doing the hand prayer and made me explain why I was doing it," Steven said. "He said that God doesn't exist and that our group is a cult."

Johnny put up his hand to calm everyone down. "It might be difficult to prove the existence of God, but it's impossible to disprove the existence of the soul. Do research work on these subjects, and then present it to your dad. If you do a good job, he won't be able to deny the existence of the soul. Then, if you prove that the soul exists, surely God exists as well."

"What subjects?" Steven asked.

"Is someone recording this?" Johnny asked.

Andy nodded and Johnny continued. "Astrology, numerology, the science of the cards, reincarnation, near-death experiences, out-of-body experiences, soul visitations, past-life regressions, indigo and crystal children, mediums, and channeling."

"Where do I learn about these?" Steven asked.

"Use the Internet and the local library," Johnny replied. "Write up a few pages on each. I'm sure you will find enough evidence to prove the existence of the soul. Anyone who exposes themselves to these subjects has to be naive to reject the existence of the soul. Once these subjects are explored, it is impossible to come away denying its existence. The proof is overwhelming."

"Can you give us some examples?" Steven asked.

"Ian Stevenson documented over ten thousand cases of reincarnation recall by children, and he is only one researcher. This isn't well publicized in the West, because it is a taboo subject and most children who remember past lives begin to forget when they are very young.

"In the East, it is much more common for people to have heard of children remembering. In the East, reincarnation is accepted as fact. For instance, the Dali Lama is selected based on his past lives, and there are people who have the ability to tap into the Akashic Records, where all of our lives are recorded.

"In the East, if you told a wise old soul that reincarnation was a fantasy, they would smile and not argue. They would consider you to be a naive young soul, who lacks wisdom. Thus, the knowledge of the soul's existence is not a belief in the East, it is knowledge that was obtained through experience."

"What else?" Steven asked.

"All of the subjects I mentioned. Just spend time doing research. They are all interesting. I'll give one more example, near-death experiences, which I think is a fascinating subject. People who have NDEs usually come back and are no longer afraid of death. In fact, most them say that death doesn't exist. Tens of thousands of people have had NDEs; some have had multiple NDEs. Most of them were not as intense as mine, where I met with an advanced being who gave me information to share with the world. But there are countless stories similar to my own. Research and write up a few of these stories. It should be compelling evidence."

Chapter Five : The Future

Julie looked at Steven. "Even if he does not believe in the existence of the soul after reading your research, he should at least have some doubt that he might be wrong. That doubt may allow you to continue coming to our group."

"I think channeling proves the existence of the soul," someone said. "Where else could that knowledge come from? There are thousands of books written using channeling. Edgar Cayce is a typical example. His channeled information from the 1920s and 1930s is still useful today. He is only one of thousands of sources that cannot be explained by science."

"Okay, everyone, let's take a seat," Johnny said. They had all been standing since Johnny and Julie walked in.

Johnny waited for everyone to find a chair. "Let me talk about the future and then I want you to talk about how your hand prayers are coming along."

Johnny scanned the room to see if everyone was ready to listen. "What I am about to tell you, only the new age movement knows about. Mainstream society has no idea about what is happening. I doubt that anyone in the government has a clue, either. The reason why is because it is too esoteric. It's hard to wrap your head around. I doubt that any of you are going to repeat this to your friends.

"First, to understand the future, you have to know the past. This planet at one time existed as a fifth-dimensional planet. This was over one hundred thousand years ago during the time of Lemuria. The Lemurians were one of the first civilizations to inhabit the planet. They were a love-based civilization. They did not have conflict or war.

"The next civilization was Atlantis, which began about one hundred thousand years ago. Its final destruction came about thirteen thousand years ago. The early Atlanteans were much like the Lemurians. However, over time, they steadily devolved and eventually, destroyed themselves. Spiritual awareness was higher during the times of Atlantis than it is today. However, their devolvement ushered in the era of the ego and individuality, and the endless wars that have occurred since that time.

"After the fall of Atlantis, it was destined that this planet would live through a very dark period for thousands of years. The Atlanteans created our destiny by turning away from the soul and embracing the ego and individuality. This is a planet of free will, so this focus on the ego was allowed. However, once the change occurred, it became very difficult to turn around. The mass consciousness turned away from the soul and instead, focused on the ego and individuality.

"While the Atlanteans were allowed to turn away from the soul and forget the truth of who they were, simultaneously, the Creator made plans to bring the truth back to humanity. These plans have been in effect since that time and are beginning to come to fruition. The achievement of that plan is almost complete.

"Starting in the late eighteen hundreds, spiritualism in the West began a rebirth. Then in the early nineteen hundreds, Theosophy and Eastern spiritual knowledge began to proliferate in the West. Alice Bailey, Rudolf Steiner, Madam Blavatsky, Jiddu Krishnamurti, Charles Leadbeater, Paramahansa Yogananda, and others began to get the word out.

"In the nineteen sixties, metaphysical knowledge exploded onto the scene in the West. John Lennon, Paul McCartney, and the Beatles even went to India to hang out with a guru. Jane Roberts became known as the woman who channeled Seth, who wrote the best-selling book Seth Speaks. Many baby boomers who were exposed to it were never the same again. A new age movement was born, and they rode that wave of spirituality to nineteen eighty-seven, when the harmonic convergence occurred. That event was huge because it impacted the collective mass consciousness, and changed the destiny of the planet. After that, more and more people began to wake up to the truth. People were learning that

Chapter Five : The Future

the soul is real, and this lifetime is a temporary illusion, just as Seth had described.

"Starting in the late nineteen eighties, the plan that had started tens of thousands of years ago began to come to fruition. The energy level of the mass consciousness began to increase and vibrate higher. It was a subtle change at first and barely noticeable, but the energy vibration began to steadily rise. A momentum had begun. Then in the nineteen nineties, the crystalline grid that surrounds the planet was realigned to support an advanced civilization that could exist in the third, fourth, and fifth dimensions simultaneously. That realignment is now completed. Soon, it will be common for people to have fourth dimensional abilities, such as telepathy, out-of-body experiences, premonitions, highly sensitive intuition, and a variety of other esoteric skills.

"Perhaps the most significant change that is coming is what I would call unity consciousness. This is what will create peace on earth. People and nations will begin to feel an affinity with one another. Today there appears to be a lot of anger, conflict, and war going on throughout the world. However, on a subconscious level, the vast majority of people are close to aligning more with love, than these other negative emotions and behaviors. This may seem impossible, but trust me, it will begin in the next decade or two. Soon people will be putting down their guns because it makes no sense for humanity to be at war with itself.

"This energy shift will transform society in a myriad of ways. Our culture, religions, economies, and politics, will all transform. How we live today will be completely replaced. The foundation of what we use for that replacement will be love and unity. That will be the core of the new civilization. And any soul that is not capable of living in such an environment will have to leave. Their soul vibration will literally be incompatible with the new energy. To be blunt, they will die of natural causes."

Johnny paused to see if anyone had a question.

"So, this grand plan was put in place to raise the vibration of the planet's mass consciousness?" someone asked.

Johnny pointed at the questioner. "Exactly. Without a higher vibration, we could not achieve peace on earth, and we could not create an advanced society that supports love and humanity."

"And this higher vibration makes it easier to become an ascended master?" another member asked.

Johnny nodded. "Yes. I was told that this is an epic opportunity for advanced souls. An opportunity that is extremely rare. That is one of the reasons why I had to come back. My soul did not want to miss this."

Julie raised her hand to ask a question and Johnny waited for her to speak. "It seems like there are two opportunities. The first one is to become an ascended master, but the other is simply to be alive during the transition into this new civilization. We are all young and could literally experience the birth of an amazing new civilization."

Everyone was quiet.

"Julie's right," Johnny said. "You will likely get to experience that birth. It's going to be quite an event. We can either stay and help with the transition, or we can ascend. But even if we do ascend, we can still help with the birth from the other side. There is going to be a lot of interaction between the new civilization and the spiritual planes. It won't be nearly as isolated as our current civilization. The veils between other dimensions won't be nearly as dense because of the rise in the energy vibration."

There was more silence.

"I see what you mean by esoteric. I don't think I could repeat this to anyone I know," someone said.

Johnny smiled. "Okay, who wants to go first telling us about their daily hand prayers?"

Chapter Five : The Future

A girl raised her hand. "I've been having good success. I meditate in my bed when I wake up in the morning for ten minutes. I start by welcoming in my spirit guides and my soul. I open up my heart and connect with them, then I let love flow between us. I ask them to guide me throughout the day.

"I open my eyes and begin the hand prayer. I look at my thumb and move it up and down. I ask myself, 'Who do I serve? The soul or the ego? I serve the soul. Today I'm going to make choices that serve the higher good.'

"Next, I move to my index finger and ask myself, 'Am I prideful or grateful? I am grateful for this lifetime, I am grateful for this opportunity?'

"Then I move my middle finger and say, 'I serve the soul through integrity and gratitude.'

"Then I move my ring finger and say, 'I maintain my integrity and gratitude by remaining heart-centered. I can trust the heart. It knows the truth. It can guide me.'

"Finally, I move my pinky and ask, 'How do you stay heart-centered? By being humble. By being kind and compassionate. By remaining calm and loving."

"Excellent," Johnny said. "Keep that up for a few months, and you will be amazed at the results. Love will begin to flow through you. I have one question. What kind of tricks is the ego trying to play to keep you from being calm, loving, and grateful?"

The girl smiled. "The ego wants me to judge others. That keeps coming up, and then I remember what you said, that we all come from the same source, and it goes away. And for some reason it wants me to watch horror films. What's that about?"

Johnny laughed. "It's trying to use fear to suck the love out of you. The ego is going to push your buttons and find ways to keep you away from unconditional love, integrity, and virtue. You have all begun an epic battle. It is a war being fought in your mind, one day at a time."

"I've been trying to keep my mind quiet and my heart open, but my mind isn't cooperating," a boy said. "It wants to think about girls, especially their bodies."

"That's a tough one," Johnny replied. "The easiest way to break that habit is to recognize that separation is an illusion. When you are thinking about them, you are pretending that they are separate from you. That is the only way the temptation has any allure. Recognize that you are both fractals of the same consciousness. Another way is to recognize that your thoughts are impinging on their lives. Remember that thoughts are energy, and they impact others in a subtle way."

"My ego wants me to constantly eat," a girl said.

"It wants you to lose your self-esteem so that it is in control," Johnny replied. "You have to get that control back. Recognize that food can be used for two purposes. The first is nourishment and the second is gratification. Learn the difference between the two and focus on nourishment. Take care of your bodies and they will take care of you. More importantly, if you take care of your bodies, it will make it much easier to have a healthy relationship with your soul."

"My ego wants me to hate someone at school," a girl said.

"The starting point of having a relationship with your soul," Johnny replied, "is recognizing that we are all one. If you perceive separation with others, then the ego is going to destroy your progress. Love cannot be conditional. It doesn't work that way. You have to love everyone without condition once you recognize that everyone is God. This is the only path for the ascended master. If you cannot hold compassion and love for others, then you are wasting your time and will fail."

Everyone was quiet.

Johnny checked the time on his phone. "Okay, that's enough for tonight. Keep up with the hand prayers, and try to keep your

Chapter Five : The Future

mind as quiet as you can throughout the day. Try to heighten your intuition by listening with your heart as much as possible."

Johnny and Julie walked out first. Many of the others hung out and talked for another hour.

* * * * *

Two weeks later, Johnny received a call from a cable television show that invited him on as a guest to be interviewed. Johnny accepted the offer, remembering his promise to share this information with society.

The interview took place one-on-one, without a studio audience. It was scheduled to be a twenty-minute segment. Johnny sat down across the table from the host and waited for the first question. He was very calm and considered the interview to be part of his duty to humanity.

"Johnny, we understand that you are in a new documentary that is coming out about near-death experiences. Can you tell us about yours?"

"Sure. I died while riding my bike when I was struck by a car. I died for about ten minutes. During that time, my soul left my body and returned to the spiritual planes of existence. I know now that these planes are our true home. This physical dimension that we live in today is an illusion. It isn't real."

The interviewer was a bit stunned by Johnny's nonchalance and calm demeanor. "How do you know that?"

"I experienced it. I experienced the soul, which is real. The human body cannot exist without the soul. Conversely, the soul has no problem existing without the human body. Once I was outside my body, I knew that I was home. It felt much more natural. The level of bliss and joy is beyond anything that we experience while in a human body."

Johnny waited for a reply.

"So, you have no doubt about the existence of the soul and the existence of the afterlife?"

Johnny grinned. "Trust me, they both exist."

"You met someone when you had your NDE, didn't you? What did they tell you?"

"This is where it gets very interesting," Johnny said, with his calm demeanor. "Many people have had NDEs and experienced the soul outside of their body. What is unique about my experience is what I was told. Or, more precisely, what I was given. Which was an abundance of knowledge."

"What were you told?" the interviewer asked.

"The meaning of life, among other things. It was downloaded to me via telepathy in a large packet of information. This information is stored in my soul's memory, and not my brain. After all, when this information was downloaded to me, I was out of my body."

"What is the meaning of life?" the interviewer asked.

"It's not what everyone wants to hear, so people will probably turn the channel after I tell you. But, here it is…. The meaning of life for humans is the evolvement of the soul. Every person on this planet is here with an agenda to increase the awareness of their soul. That's why we are here. The soul is striving to remember who and what it is, which is a fractal of consciousness of the Creator."

Johnny stopped and waited.

"A fractal?" the interviewer said in a disbelieving tone.

"It's just a term. We are each a tiny piece of consciousness of the Creator."

"You said that we are striving to remember? It's more complicated than that, isn't it?" the interviewer asked.

Johnny nodded. "Indeed, it's extremely complex. But let's keep it simple, since we only have twenty minutes. Let me talk a little bit about the soul. I was given immense knowledge about the soul,

Chapter Five : The Future

and it is quite fascinating. The soul is connected to the source, to the Creator. Right now, my soul extends out of this room and connects to the source. So does yours and everyone else's in this studio. Do you understand what this means? We are all connected. And we are all one."

"These are big concepts," the interviewer said. "First, you tell us that the soul exists. Then you tell us it is connected to the source, to the Creator."

"There is more," Johnny said, brushing off the interviewer's skepticism. "If people knew the truth, they would reorganize society tomorrow. The only thing that is real on this planet is the soul, and the soul is eternal. We thought that Jesus was special because he was perceived as the son of God. When in actuality, we are all the sons of God. We are all the same as Jesus; he was just a bit more evolved. And that is why we are here, to become evolved like he was."

"Are you a Christian?"

"No, I'm a gnostic, although Jesus was also a gnostic. A gnostic is someone who knows that the soul exists. We don't live by the belief in God, we already know that God exists. Perhaps five percent of the population are gnostics, but that number is growing rapidly."

"Tell me more about this truth that can change the world?" the interviewer asked.

"Well, I've already told you the important points, but I can tell you some more. This dimension where we now live is the lowest dimension, also called the third dimension. It was created for only one purpose, which is to be a school for the soul. You see, in the third dimension you can forget who you are. This creates an opportunity for the soul to enter a fantasy world that appears to be real. It is the ultimate illusion, the ultimate simulation."

"But why is it necessary?" the interviewer continued with his skeptical tone.

"It is the only way for the soul to evolve. You have to experience pain to know pain. You have to experience sorrow to know sorrow. You have to experience cruelty to know cruelty. And on and on. On the higher spiritual planes, these experiences are not possible because all that exists is harmony and unity."

"You're implying that the world is a simulation and that it is not real."

Johnny nodded. "That's right, although it is a simulation that is extremely complex. For instance, we each live thousands of lifetimes experiencing whatever the soul needs, while at the same time working in conjunction with other souls to help each other become more spiritually aware. Most souls on this planet have no idea why they are here and what they are trying to achieve. Very few even try to find out. Most people simply live their lives with blinders on and learn the lessons they came to learn. They don't question reality. Those people aren't watching this show, or they've already turned the channel."

"Do you mean that we can find answers about the nature of reality? We can find the truth about our existence?" For the first time, the interviewer actually seemed interested.

Johnny nodded. "Not only can you find answers, but if people knew that their thoughts and actions were impacting their future lives, they would be living a lot differently. For instance, how we live in this lifetime impacts our subsequent lives. It's a lot like preparing to get into an elite college. Today, only about five percent of the applicants get into Stanford University. We are all vying for spots in future lives, and there are only so many spots. If you knew that, you would live your life a lot differently."

"What do you mean by spots?"

"Today there are about six billion souls incarnated on this planet. The truth is that there are billions more souls who would like to be here at this time. It is an epic time to be alive because of the changes that are coming. Those souls who are here achieved

Chapter Five : The Future

their lifetimes, or spots, from past choices and experiences. Those who get to reincarnate back to this planet will be a select group, much like the next Stanford freshman class."

"And those people who find their soul will get to come back?"

"Many of them, yes. You will increase your odds dramatically if you find it and serve it."

"How do we do that?"

"How much time do we have left in the interview?" Johnny smiled.

"About ten minutes."

"Okay, that's plenty of time. The key is looking within and finding your soul. If you can find it, then you can find out why you are here. Your soul will tell you. Normally, access to the soul on this planet would be limited to about one or two percent of the population. This is because of the density of the energy vibration in this dimension. All physical matter, which is made up of electrons and protons, and other particles, is energy vibrating. Only the soul is pure energy, which vibrates at a much faster rate than physical matter and is indestructible. The physical body vibrates at about 100,000 cycles per second. The soul vibrates even faster.

"Starting in the nineteen sixties, the dense energy vibration on the planet started increasing at a quicker pace. Rock and roll was born, and the world has never been quite the same. As the planet's energy vibrates higher, so do our bodies. Once we reach an average of around 120,000 cycles per second, we will have peace on earth. The energy vibration has now reached a level where as many as twenty-five percent of the global population can access their soul, and it's increasing every day."

"How?" the interviewer asked incredulously.

"You do this by understanding that the core of the soul is the face of God. In fact, it is God, and the basis of our existence. The core exists as purity, unconditional love, and compassion for humankind. Once you know what the soul is, you can begin to expose it by marginalizing the ego. The ego is the opposite of these virtues, this is why it is so difficult to find the soul. The ego literally gets in the way and blocks it. The ego is always doing something that is self-serving, something to achieve its definition of happiness. To counteract this, you have to learn how to serve the soul instead of the ego. You have to access your heart-center.

"Ironically, humans tend to think that God gave us this lifetime as a gift to do with as we please. And that it is our prerogative to do whatever makes us happy. This is the essence of pride. If there is one thing religions have gotten right, it is that the sin of pride is the worst sin of all. We even know the story of Satan, who was supposedly thrown out of heaven for refusing to serve God. Yet, here we all are, serving the ego. This is the exact reason Satan was condemned."

"Is that why monks live in monasteries? To avoid the temptations of the ego and the sin of pride?"

"Yes, for some monks that is true. They want to avoid the temptations of the world. I should note that some monks do find their soul in monasteries and ashrams."

"Could I find my soul?" the interviewer asked, with a tone of skepticism.

"Sure. Some people are fortunate to have an esoteric experience, where the soul exposes itself. Once this happens, people are never the same again. This often occurs during an NDE (near-death experience) or an OBE (out-of-body experience). However, for most people, you have to become heart-centered to find the soul. You have to become like-minded with the soul. Think of the ultimate integrity and the ultimate unconditional love, and that is the soul. We have to become somewhat like that to find it. And with the ego as our nemesis, it becomes very difficult.

"I teach people how to find their soul using a hand prayer that I developed. It's on my website, and you can email me with questions if you have trouble understanding it. I'm confident that if

Chapter Five : The Future

you do the hand prayer for a few months, you will find your soul. However, once you find it, the real challenge begins. I think that finding your soul can be easy for many people now that the energy vibration has increased. What is not so easy, is marginalizing the ego and serving the soul on a daily basis. The ego will do everything it can to retain its dominant position. It knows your weaknesses, and it knows how to push your buttons."

"Temptation is everywhere."

Johnny nodded. "Exactly. The ego knows how to tempt us. But if we want to live by the truth, then we have to marginalize that temptation and serve the soul instead. We have to become virtuous and gracious, which is not easily done. And if you succeed, there is a huge reward."

"Which is?"

"You become an ascended master. That is what we are all trying to obtain, although perhaps not in this lifetime. Until it is achieved, we are all apprentices in training. What we would all like to do is graduate, but it's not easy."

The interviewer's eyes lit up. "I think I just had an epiphany. Let me see if I have this right. The Creator created this third dimensional simulation that allows souls to evolve. However, this evolvement is extremely difficult, and the key to this evolvement is finding the truth. And this truth is hidden inside of us, where we have to look for it. Am I right so far?"

Johnny nodded.

"If that's all true, then the key to finding this truth is desire. At some point in our evolvement, we begin to recognize what has more value, the truth or egotistical satisfaction. Our desire eventually turns to searching for the truth. We eventually look inside and find the truth, where it was hiding all along."

Johnny smiled. "Bravo. Are you ready to start?"

The interviewer smiled. "No, I'm not ready to give up my Porsche and my lifestyle. Marginalizing the ego doesn't sound too easy, or much fun. Perhaps in my next life."

Johnny laughed. "Don't worry. You'll get another chance. Eventually, your desire to drive fast will fade."

Chapter Six

THREE SYSTEMS

Julie knocked on the front door of Johnny's house. She had become a regular visitor and the Randall's were always happy to see her.

"Hello Mr. Randall. How are you today?" Julie said as she walked in through the open door.

"I'm fine, Julie. Johnny is upstairs."

"Thanks," she said, as she headed up the stairs.

She opened Johnny's bedroom door without knocking. He was sitting at his desk using his computer.

Johnny glanced back at Julie. "Hi," he said, before returning his focus to the computer.

"I need a few minutes to finish this post," he said.

She laid down on his bed. "That's fine. I can wait."

"Did you have dinner yet?" Johnny asked.

"Yeah, me and my sister ordered out. You?"

"Yeah," Johnny replied, without looking up.

Julie laid back and stared at the ceiling. "I've been thinking about what you said last night. I want you to tell me about some of those subjects you mentioned that prove the existence of the soul. Except for out-of-body experiences. I know that one."

Johnny glanced at Julie. "Which one do you want to talk about?"

"I guess we can start at the top of the list and work down. I brought my notepad."

Johnny looked at Julie and saw that she, indeed, had brought a notebook along with a pen. "Which topic is at the top?"

Julie opened the notebook and said, "Astrology is first."

Johnny finished his post and closed the cover of his laptop. He remained seated in his computer chair and turned around to face Julie. "Do you have a birth certificate?"

"I think so. I'll have to ask my mom."

"We will need it to find out what time you were born. That will give us your rising sign. I have a computer program that prints out a thirty-page report of your natal chart."

"My what?" Julie asked incredulously.

"Your natal chart? It's a snapshot of the planets, the Moon, and the Sun when you took your first breath. It reveals your personality traits."

Johnny got up and opened a cabinet drawer. He reached down and removed a large manila envelope.

"Here's mine," he said, handing Julie his natal chart.

She opened the envelope and started reading.

"Nostradamus never told anyone his birthday or time of birth," Johnny said. "He knew how accurate astrology was and wanted to guard his privacy. He was an excellent astrologer. Astrology is so old that we don't know its origins. It seems like it has always been around. The truth is that it came from Atlantis and is an ancient science."

"I'm lost," Julie said. "What am I reading."

"It's highly complex. If you really want to learn astrology, it will take a minimum of a few months, and some people study for years before they consider themselves a professional astrologer."

"I just want to learn enough to know what it's about," Julie said.

"Okay, we'll go over the basics. Each planet, the Moon, and the Sun are located somewhere on your chart. The location of each one tells you something about yourself. For instance, a chart is broken into twelve sections, called houses. Each of these is associated with an astrological sign, depending on the time and place you were born.

"The first house is your rising sign. I'm a Cancer rising, so that is my first house. In my chart, all of the subsequent houses follow Cancer. The second house is Leo, the third is Virgo, and so on, until you reach the twelfth house. The location of the planets, the Moon, and the Sun in your houses is determined by when and where you took your first breath.

"I have the Sun in Pisces. This single piece of information tells you a lot about me, but there is much, much more to decipher from the chart. Pisces is a water sign; this makes me sensitive and in touch with my feelings. I'm much more inclined to be led by my feelings instead of my logical mind. All Pisces' tend to be emotionally soft people, because of their sensitive side. Conversely, if my Sun sign was in Gemini, I would be more driven by my logical mind, because Gemini is an air sign."

Johnny paused, but Julie was too busy writing notes to ask a question.

"Also, since the Sun is in the tenth house, my parents can relax and not worry about me. I will be ambitious and driven to accomplish goals. I'm not going to be lazy or accept failure. It's a very good place to have your Sun sign in this competitive world that we live in today."

"What else can you tell me about your Sun sign?" Julie asked.

"Each astrological sign has an element and a quality. The elements are earth, water, fire, and air. The qualities are cardinal, fixed, and mutable. Once you know the descriptions of each, you can get a better understanding of how astrology works, and what drives people's behavior. For instance, I'm a Pisces, which is a water element and a mutable quality. This means I can change much easier than a fixed sign. People born under fixed signs can be quite stubborn.

"Natal charts are incredibly accurate describing someone because you can add up how many planets, along with the Sun and Moon, that are in the various elements and qualities. I have mostly water signs, which says a lot about me. If I had mostly air, earth, or fire, then I would have a completely different personality."

"Wait," Julie said, to make Johnny pause. "Do you mean that when and where you are born determines your personality?"

"Absolutely," Johnny replied. "Give me someone's natal chart and I can tell you more about that person than they probably know about themselves. What is really cool is combining astrology, numerology, and the science of the cards to get a clear picture of someone. It's amazingly accurate."

"Tell me more," Julie said.

"Each house has a specific description. So, any astrological sign, or planet in a house, can tell you something about that person. For instance, the first house tells us about someone's personality and temperament. I have Cancer in my first house, so I am family oriented, and my emotions change quite frequently. This is because Cancer is ruled by the Moon."

"Ruled by what? You lost me," Julie said, scribbling down notes as fast as she could.

"You have to read the descriptions of each astrological sign, along with the descriptions of each planet and the Sun and Moon. Pisces is ruled by Neptune. So, to understand Pisces, you have to read the astrological description of Neptune. The short version is that Neptune is the dreamy, creative, and artistic planet. People with this influence can be extremely imaginative and creative. You can have this influence in your chart if you have planets, the Moon, the Sun, or rising sign in Pisces."

"My brain is not grasping this," Julie said. "This is too much information to absorb at one time."

Johnny smiled. "It's a science and it takes some time to learn."

"Unless you get it downloaded all at once!" Julie exclaimed.

Johnny laughed.

Chapter Six : Three Systems

"Before we stop talking about astrology," Julie said, "I want to talk about the impact of the time and place of someone's birth."

"Sure," Johnny replied.

"If astrology is real, and from what I'm hearing, it clearly is, then this is how we choose our lifetimes. We can choose the personality that we need to learn our lessons. This also implies that the time of conception is planned in advance. Is that true?"

"Absolutely," Johnny replied. "Once a family is formed, the souls that want to be born will influence when they are born. In fact, most children not only pick the time and place of their birth, but also their name. Our name impacts our numerology. Everything has energy, including our names. I'm going to have to change my name to John pretty soon, because it vibrates higher and will help with my ascension. I think I'm going to wait until I graduate from high school."

"Okay, then let's talk about numerology," Julie said, turning the page in her notebook.

"Sure," Johnny said.

"By the way, I'm taking your natal chart home with me tonight. I want to read it."

"That's fine," Johnny replied. "You can keep it. I can print another one. And once you get your birth certificate, text me your birth time and city. I already know your birthday, May twelfth. You are a seven of diamonds. I'm a five of diamonds, so we are a good match."

Julie laughed. "I'm a what? You always say things that I'm expected to know."

"Your birthday determines your card in the science of the cards. We can talk about that after numerology."

"Okay. Is a seven of diamonds a good card?"

Johnny nodded. "Yeah, it's a really good card to have. Better than mine. I can see why you can travel out of your body."

"What's numerology?" Julie asked, getting ready to take notes.

"It's basically energy from numbers that can impact our lives quite dramatically. Everyone has six main numbers, which are your lifepath number, birthday number, attitude number, personality number, soul number, and power number. These numbers are crucial for relationships, but they can impact a great many events in our lives, because nearly anything can have its own numerology, including houses, businesses, organizations, governments, even pets.

"The father of numerology is Pythagoras. He was the first to define the energy of each number and letter, and give them descriptions. Once you know your numbers, you can go and look them up for meanings.

"The most important number is your lifepath, which is your birthdate. Add up all the digits in your birthdate, which are the year and day. If the total is two digits, then add those together, until it reduces to one. My birthday digits add up to twenty-eight, which combines to a ten, and finally, one. So, I am a twenty-eight, one. I can then look up the information that describes the lifepath for someone who is a twenty-eight, one. When you combine this with a natal chart, the dots begin to connect.

"Your birthday number is your birth day combined into one number.

"Your attitude number is your birth month and birth day combined into one number.

"Your personality number is the consonants in your full name combined into one number.

"Your soul number is the vowels in your full name combined into one number.

"Your power number is the combination of the personality and soul number combined into one number.

"Because you can change your name, you can literally change your energy."

Chapter Six : Three Systems

"That's why you want to change to John?" Julie asked.

Johnny nodded. "Yeah, it will change three of my numbers."

"You said that it was crucial for relationships? What did you mean?" Julie asked.

"Not only are some numbers more compatible than others, but some are incompatible to each other. This is the Creator's way of creating drama and a diversity of experiences."

"What do you mean by incompatible?"

"It's like oil and water. Some numbers just don't mix. This is why, when you meet people, sometimes you feel this warm feeling of compatibility, and at other times you do not. That is energy you are feeling, and numbers are a good way of measuring the energy of a person."

"How do letters turn into numbers?" Julie asked, as she jotted down another note.

"Pythagorus gave each letter a number. For instance, an M is a 4, a K is a 2, an S is a 1. There doesn't seem to make any sense to the values, but it works."

"So, you are saying that people whose numbers are incompatible should never marry?"

Johnny laughed. "Yes. Unless they want to fight a lot and be miserable."

"And you can determine this incompatibility?" Julie asked, intrigued.

Johnny nodded. "It's quite easy. If you only have one or no compatible numbers, then you are not compatible. And if you only have two, then you better have a fairly good connection with your natal chart or your card. It is best to have at least three compatible numbers if you want to get married."

"But how do you determine if a number is not compatible?" Julie asked.

"Each person has six numbers, and each type of number can be checked for compatibility. For instance, my lifepath is a one. If your lifepath is a four, six, or eight, then our lifepath numbers are not compatible. That leaves us with five more chances to find compatibility in some of our other numbers."

Julie nodded, while she quickly scribbled down notes.

"There are two types of compatible numbers. The first type is considered a natural match and is the most compatible. For me, I have a lot of ones, threes, and fives. If you have a lot of ones, threes, and fives, then we will likely be highly compatible. The second type is considered to be compatible, but not as strongly as a natural match. For me, it is twos, threes, and nines. I tend to get along fine with people who have those six numbers."

"And people without them tend to be challenging for you?"

Johnny nodded. "Yes, a connection seems to be missing."

"How do I find out my six numbers?" Julie asked.

"It's easy. All you need is the Pythagoras letter conversions, which are on the Internet."

"Should I include my middle name?"

Johnny shook his head. "No, use the name you go by. That's the energy that people know you by."

"If we got married, could my new name be incompatible?" Julie asked, with concern.

"Yes, that's true. People should be careful whenever they change their name. But we could make sure that your new name doesn't cause a problem by checking the impact of a name change. You possibly could keep your last name and hyphenate it with mine. If the universe wants us together, then it will be compatible.

Julie smiled. "I hope so. Now, tell me about the science of the cards."

Chapter Six : Three Systems

"This is my favorite one for determining someone's personality. Everyone's card fits like a glove. I'm a five of diamonds, and I match nearly all of its traits."

Johnny reached for his iPad. He tapped a few times on the screen and handed it to Julie.

"Here, read this."

Julie put the iPad down on the bed. She started reading and scrolled down every few seconds.

"That does fit you."

"Now read you," Johnny said.

He pointed to the "find a card link," and Julie found her card and started reading.

"That's crazy," she said. "How can it be so accurate? Is it like this for everyone?"

Johnny nodded. "And very few people know about it."

"How could something so powerful be unknown?"

Johnny shrugged. "All I know is that esoteric knowledge has been ignored by mainstream society. If you look at the common perception of astrology, numerology, and the science of the cards, you will see that there has been a longstanding pattern of intransigence and skepticism. Most scholars refuse to even consider them as authentic. This is strange, because anyone who does any research quickly recognizes that they are real. But if you ask a random person on the street, they will say they are fake. More people believe in reincarnation than astrology and numerology."

"Where did the science of the cards come from?" Julie asked.

"No one knows. It's another ancient knowledge that has an unknown origin. I think it can be more difficult to learn than astrology because you have to learn all fifty-two cards. It can be used for divination and is an extremely complex system. You can use it for predicting future events, even what you will experience tomorrow or next week. It can also be used for finding compatibility between people."

"That's fascinating. I should try to learn one of the three systems," Julie said.

"I would do the science of the cards. It will take an incredible amount of work, but it is a very powerful system, once you learn it. And I think it is better at predicting the future than astrology."

"Okay, I'm out of time," Julie said, closing her notepad.

"I thought we were going to make out," Johnny said.

"Nope, all you get is a kiss goodnight."

"Bummer!"

"There's always tomorrow," Julie said, as she kissed him goodnight.

Chapter Seven

GOD'S VIRTUES

Julie's mom knocked on her bedroom door and then walked in. "We need to talk, Julie."

Julie was lying on her bed, reading. She looked up at her mother. "What about?"

"Johnny Randall. You two have been inseparable for the past few months. I called his parents, and they confirmed my suspicion."

Julie became angry. "Why did you call them?"

"I'm concerned. I haven't seen any of your friends all summer. What have you been doing with Johnny?"

"My personal life is none of your business," Julie said.

"Oh, yes, it is! I'm your mother. Hand me the book you're reading."

Julie did as her mother demanded and handed her the book.

"What is this?" She turned the book over to read the back cover.

"It's a channeled book from the Arcturians," Julie replied.

"I don't want you reading this," her mother said. "It's not real and will only confuse you, or worse."

"Oh, mother. You don't know what you are talking about. The Arcturians are an advanced race who are educating us on spirituality and how we should live. It's extremely valuable knowledge."

"Since when did you start talking like this? I'm concerned about your relationship with Johnny."

"He's my boyfriend, and I am not going to stop seeing him."

"We'll see about that!" her mother replied harshly, as she turned to leave.

* * * * *

Driving to the meetup group, Julie told Johnny about the incident with her mother.

"We might have a problem," Julie said.

"What do you mean?" Johnny asked.

"My mother found me reading a channeled book, and she thinks you are a bad influence. I think she wants me to stop seeing you."

Johnny hesitated. "What are you going to do?"

"Nothing. They can't keep us apart. I only have two more years of high school, and then, I'm a free adult."

"I should come over and talk to your parents," Johnny said.

"Are you going to tell them about the NDE?"

"Yes, I have to tell them who I have become. I have to tell the truth. If that doesn't work, then they probably will tell you that I am no longer welcome at your house."

Julie hesitated. "Let's wait and see how my father responds. He might persuade my mom to back off."

Johnny nodded.

* * * * *

When Johnny and Julie walked in to the meetup group, the other eighteen members were already seated and excited to learn more about the soul. Julie found a seat, and Johnny remained standing in front of the room.

Johnny started pointing at each member as he counted the number of people in attendance.

"Everyone is here, so let's begin. Tonight, I'm going to talk about living God's virtues and self-mastery. As I have told you before, the energy field on the planet is changing. The vibrational frequency is getting higher and continues to increase. These higher

Chapter Seven : God's Virtues

frequencies allow us to access our soul. You can use an analogy of the bandwidth used to access the Internet. Currently, we have dial-up access to our soul, but soon we will have cable access, and eventually, fiber access.

"With our dial-up access, we can begin to change the way we live. Dial-up is limited and is not a full-blown communication channel, but we can still feel and hear guidance. This channel is open, and it provides access to the soul, and with this access, the truth is exposed, and guidance is possible...."

"How is the truth exposed?" someone interrupted.

"The truth is that our true self is aligned with God's virtues of unconditional love, compassion, non-judgment, and higher purpose. This truth can be obtained by tapping into your soul and living your highest truth. Your soul will give you guidance in showing you that truth.

"Once you find this truth, you will recognize that nothing happens without a higher purpose. This is why judgment is never needed. God always has a plan for every action, which is beyond our understanding or comprehension. Instead of us trying to determine what is right and wrong for either ourselves or others, it is for us to live every moment focused on living for the highest good with God's virtues guiding us."

Someone raised their hand, and Johnny pointed to them.

"It's a reinforcing loop, isn't it? The more we live by these virtues, the more the soul gives us guidance."

Johnny nodded. "Yes. The more you follow these virtues, the more you will feel the soul's influence in your life. As your heart expands through the unconditional love of humanity, you will feel your soul in your heart. You will become much more feeling oriented. After a while, the soul will be as involved in your life as the ego used to be. This time, however, instead of your head giving you guidance, you will begin to feel the guidance from your heart.

"The more we align with these virtues, the more we shine our light out to humanity. Thus, the more we align, the more we shine. This is our daily goal."

"Can you give us some examples?" someone asked.

"Sure, you will come home from school, and your sister or brother will have a sad look on their face. You will feel a strong urge to be of help, and you do what you can to cheer them up. This is from the virtue of empathy. Your intentions will be pure and unconditional. Another situation may occur at school when someone is bullied or verbally attacked. Because of the virtue of compassion, you will feel compelled to offer assistance in any way that you can.

"These are examples of living a spiritual life that is driven by God's virtues, and spreading your light to humanity. Every moment of your life should be spent living for the highest good. Once your soul knows that this is your lifestyle, it will do everything it can to support you and give you guidance. Your intent and beliefs are very powerful influences on what you will experience in your life. Your life is not happening by accident. You are creating it. Trust me when I say that your soul will be there to guide you and will make itself known to you. That dial-up channel may be limited, but the soul will find a way to communicate."

Someone raised their hand and Johnny pointed.

"I've read that if we keep our minds quiet, it is easier to communicate with the soul."

Johnny nodded. "Absolutely. This is why meditating is so helpful, but ultimately, you want to meditate at all times, keeping your mind quiet. I love it when my soul talks to me and tells me things. It's almost like another friend. Last night, it told me that it was dinner time."

Several people laughed.

"The soul tells me things like that all the time. The moment before my phone rings, I will think of someone and know it is them

Chapter Seven : God's Virtues

calling. My mom will have to work late, and I know it before my dad tells me. I know these things before they happen because there is a connection between all of life. And it is the soul that creates that connection."

"So, your soul talks to you?" someone asked.

"Yes, although it could also be my spirit guides," Johnny replied. "Both are looking out for my interests, so I don't try to determine which one it is. My spirit guides are my guardian angels. I call them spirit guides because they are not always angels. We always have at least one spirit guide with us at all time, and sometimes we have several. I've had one spirit guide with me since birth, and he is not an angel. He's a regular soul, just like you and me. Angels, on the other hand, have never incarnated."

Julie raised her hand. "Johnny, are you implying that the more virtuous we become, the closer the relationship we will have with our soul and spirit guides?"

Johnny nodded. "Absolutely, but your virtuousness must be done in tandem with a quiet mind and a spiritual path. If you are virtuous, but play computer games all day long, that is not going to work very well to communicate with your soul."

A few people laughed.

"Let me explain the goal that we are all trying to achieve. We want to open a clear channel with our soul so that it can guide us at all times. This channel is at its best when our mind is quiet. Our higher self knows what we need to do, and it will lead us in subtle ways. We will be guided on what to do and what to avoid. Our lives should manifest in a harmonious way if we listen to the soul. And if our lives go astray, all we need to do is listen to the silence. Whatever feels right, is going to be the right way. You can trust the heart. It is always right."

"I think I understand what you are teaching us," someone said. "If we awaken each morning and do the hand prayer, and then live each moment for the highest good, using the virtues of God, then the soul will give us guidance."

Johnny nodded. "Excellent. Who wants to mention some of the things he left out?"

"Keep the mind quiet," someone said.

"Non-judgment and unconditional love," said another.

"Create harmony in your life," said another.

"Pay attention to the soul's guidance," said another.

"Expand your heart to allow unconditional love to flow," said another.

"Love all of humanity," said another.

"Love is all that matters," said another.

"Live in the now, connected to your soul," said another.

"Live for the highest truth," said another.

"Everything that occurs in life has a higher purpose," said another.

"Accept everything that happens as a blessing or opportunity,' said another.

"As the frequencies increase, our consciousness expands and exposes the soul," said another.

"As the frequencies increase, the truth is exposed," said another.

"Our motives should be to help humanity," said another.

"We should have no enemies," said another.

"Becoming an ascended master is about integrating the virtues of God into this lifetime," said another.

"Remain neutral using a frequency of love," said another.

Johnny waited until there was five seconds of silence, and everyone had a chance to speak.

"Excellent answers," Johnny said. "You are a fine group of initiates. Now, I want to discuss self-mastery, which is required to become an ascended master. Self-mastery is the ability to control your thoughts and emotions, and to keep them centered on

Chapter Seven : God's Virtues

God's virtues. These include love of your soul, love of humanity, compassion, empathy, sincerity, honesty, calmness, and gentleness. This is the hardest thing to learn, because the ego wants to be in control, and it uses the mind to distract you...."

"So," someone interrupted, "self-mastery is the ability to avoid egotistical thoughts, or thoughts that run counter to God's virtues."

Johnny thought for a moment. "Yes, but self-mastery is more than that. It is a lifestyle that acknowledges that you have made a commitment to the Creator and to your higher self that you will serve humanity. It is a sacred vow to serve the Creator, the soul, and humanity. Self-mastery is living that vow. It is living a life focused on this vow, with a commitment and desire that is manifested through your thoughts and actions."

Someone let out a deep breath from the recognition of what that statement implied.

"In many respects," Johnny continued, "most people are just like Satan. He turned his back on his sacred vow to serve the Creator. He rejected service to humanity and chose self-gratification. His sin was pride, which is ours as well. Today, we have forgotten our vows. Self-mastery is a return to those vows. It is the elimination of egotistical pride and the return of a willingness to serve, a willingness to be humble and walk in humility."

"That's what you were told?" Julie asked, confused by this talk of Satan and sacred vows.

"Yes, and what is happening today is that we are turning within to find the truth. We are doing this to re-integrate with our soul in order to serve God. We are re-discovering our sacred vows that we are here to share our love with all of humanity. We are turning away from the duality of the external world, toward the singularity of the inner world."

"Why do I need a vow, when the truth will suffice?" Julie asked.

"They are one and the same," Johnny replied. "There is nothing written or said that formalizes our sacred vows. It is more like the love a mother has for her child. She vows to take care of the child. It is her responsibility. That is her sacred vow when she gives birth."

Julie smiled. "That makes more sense. Now I understand what you mean. I was having a hard time processing it."

"Self-mastery is a return to the integrity of our true self. It is a spiritual lifestyle that removes negativity and adds positive traits. It leads to an expansion of love, and a strengthening of our etheric field. Our soul literally gets stronger and more powerful as it vibrates higher.

"For instance, when an obstacle appears in our life, which can be anything that appears to disrupt our harmony, we have the ability to recognize that the obstacle is simply a blessing or an opportunity. It has appeared for our benefit. It is our prerogative to not allow the obstacle to disrupt or impact our spiritual journey. Self-mastery gives us the ability to deal with obstacles."

Johnny paused and waited for a question.

"How does our soul get stronger?" someone asked.

"As our spiritual awareness increases, so does our soul vibration. We literally shine as a more luminous light. The purer our thoughts and the more integrated we become with our soul, the more luminous we become. Conversely, if we lose our commitment to serve, our soul can fragment and lose its strength. Alcohol, drugs, anger, and even a poor diet can fragment the soul's etheric field. Anything that is contrary to God's virtues can impact it."

"So, let me see if I got this right," someone said. "If we live with self-mastery, which means controlling our thoughts and actions by following God's virtues, then we can integrate closely with our soul and increase our light body with an expansion of love."

"Excellent. Who wants to add something?" Johnny said with a grin, knowing he would get a lot of good answers.

"Not serving is an egotistical act," someone said.

"We have a commitment to our soul and to each other," said another.

"We are guardians of truth," said another.

"Love of humanity and love of self is the foundation of God's virtues," said another.

"Life is a journey into higher consciousness, awareness, and understanding," said another.

"As duality begins to break down, peace becomes possible," said another.

"The journey is not about obstacles; instead, it is about service," said another.

"Ascension is about adding light to our etheric light body," said another.

"Obstacles are illusions," said another.

"Serve gently, with love," said another.

"The more deeply integrated with our soul, the more powerful we become," said another.

"Obstacles do not have to impact our journey," said another.

"Conflict does not have to exist," said another.

"Negative thoughts and actions fragment the soul," said another.

Johnny waited until there was a long silence, and everyone had a chance to speak.

"Excellent. Okay, one last thing, and we will be done tonight. Steven, tell us how your research is coming to prove the existence of the soul. Perhaps we can give you some feedback and help in some way."

Steven hesitated, organizing his thoughts. "I started with reincarnation and past life regressions. There is an amazing amount of information. I went to the library and brought home ten books because that was all I could carry."

Several people laughed.

"I've been reading them and taking notes. Ian Stevenson's material is rock solid. He focuses on young children who have been able to prove that they lived before. In one case, a young boy identified a man who murdered him in a past life. He had a scar from the incident, and the murderer confessed when confronted by the boy.

"There are dozens and dozens of similar cases where children have very high recall. Children will remember the towns where they lived and many of the people whom they knew from a past life. The children sometimes go back to these towns and then have conversations with these people, using their past life memories."

"I know a story you should check out," someone said. "There was a boy who remembered being an American fighter pilot in World War Two. He flew against the Japanese in the Pacific. His memories were so clear that he knew his past life name and the names of the people he flew with. He knew precise details about the plane he flew, even though he had no exposure to any knowledge about the plane. He went to a reunion with the survivors of his air unit and remembered some of the people. If you Google 'American fighter pilot reincarnation,' you will find it."

"A lot of the Crystal children remember their past lives," someone said. "You should check that out."

"Who are the Crystal children?" someone asked.

"They came in after the Indigo children," Johnny said. "The Indigos started arriving in the nineteen seventies. Then they began to come in large numbers, from the late nineteen eighties to the late nineteen nineties. The Crystals started arriving in the mid nineteen nineties and continue to arrive.

"The Indigos are considered system busters. They are very strong-willed and highly intelligent. They are fearless and extremely creative. Often, their parents and society cannot handle them because they are usually smarter than adults. They do not like to be told what to do and revere their freedom. They tend to be psychic and have a deep inner knowing about life. One of their pet peeves is that they demand to be respected because they have a high sense of self-worth. They also have old soul wisdom, and it's normal for them to have anti-social behavior.

"The Crystals are much more angelic than the Indigos. They are more love-based and social. They are here to serve and are often healers of some sort. Like the Indigos, they tend to be psychic, and many of them are telepathic and can read minds. They have a deep connection to spirit and the truth. Many of them are walking angels. They make the best children, and parents of Crystals know how fortunate they are to have them. The love they exude and the love that flows from them to others is what is changing the planet. They are literally healing this civilization."

"I think I'm a Crystal," someone said.

"Me too," said another.

"And me," said another.

Johnny laughed. "Yes, most of us are Crystals. One way you can tell if you are Crystal is your reaction when you go into a new age store that sells crystals. The first time I went into a new age store that had a lot crystals, I didn't want to leave. I wanted to touch or hold every stone in the shop."

"Why do we like crystal stones so much?" someone asked.

"Because our vibration is close to crystalline," Johnny replied. "The stones are literally alive, and we can feel it. The energy grid on the planet is also crystalline. This is how consciousness transmits information. And each crystal stone can hold both consciousness and information. In fact, these crystals can be used for healing, as the consciousness of the stones is transferred into our consciousness to balance our energy."

"I have crystals all over my room," one of the girls said. "They talk to me when I can't sleep."

Johnny laughed. "Crystal children have high energy from their high vibration. For this reason, many of them do not need very much sleep."

"Now you tell me!" Julie exclaimed. "I thought I had a sleeping disorder."

Everyone laughed.

"I'm confused," Steven said. "How can the Indigo and Crystal children prove the existence of the soul?"

"From their psychic ability," Johnny replied. "Many of them can use telepathy with other children at long distances. Also, they are often adept at out-of-body experiences. Both of these skills prove the existence of the soul."

"And don't forget their ability to remember past lives," someone added.

"Steven, tell us what you found regarding past life regression," Johnny requested.

"It's quite common," Steven replied. "There are hypnotherapists in practically every city, and many large cities have hundreds. There might be as many professional hypnotherapists as professional astrologers. They are everywhere. Not all of them do past life regressions, but many do. I especially like the work of Dolores Cannon. Her series of books on *The Convoluted Universe* is stunning. All of the information in her books comes from people regressed into past lives."

"Make sure to check the work of Michael Newton," someone said. "He has shown that hypnotic regression can be used to heal a variety of psychological ailments. It seems like we bring baggage from past lives into this life. And that once we understand where the baggage came from, it goes away. He has helped many people using this technique."

"And don't forget his book, *Journey of Souls*, which is on our reading list. It is, perhaps, the definitive book on how reincarnation works," someone added.

"The first chapter of that book should be required reading for everyone on the planet," Johnny said. "It will either wake you up to the truth, or you will never wake up. You are either ready for it, or you are not. How many of you have read it?"

About half of the members raised their hands.

"After the rest of you read it, we can discuss it in detail. It's one of my favorite books. It describes how the soul plans its lifetimes. If that doesn't get your interest, then I don't know what will."

Johnny looked at the members. Everyone looked back with anticipation and a keen interest.

"That's it for tonight. Next month, you are going to speak about how your life has changed since you began doing the hand prayer. So, come prepared to talk about your life. I'll see you next month."

Johnny headed for the door. As usual, Johnny and Julie did not stay and were the first to walk out. Most of the other meetup members stayed and hung out. They were all becoming close friends.

Chapter Eight

THE TRUTH SHALL SET YOU FREE

Johnny knocked on the front door of Julie's house. He was extremely nervous because he didn't know what the outcome was going to be.

Julie's father answered the door. "Come in, Johnny."

Her father didn't smile, but Johnny didn't feel any animosity. Johnny relaxed, as he followed her father into the house. Julie and her mother were seated in the living room, waiting.

Johnny sat down. "Hello, Mrs. Davis."

"Hello, Johnny. Thank you for coming," she replied.

"Johnny, our daughter has asked us to let you explain your relationship with her. We would like you to be as candid and honest as you can be."

Johnny nodded. "Before I begin explaining, and thank you for giving me this opportunity, I would like you to watch an interview that I recently gave."

Johnny was holding a DVD case in one of his hands. It was the documentary about NDEs.

"Sure, we could do that," her father replied.

He got up and took the DVD from Johnny and walked over to the television. He picked up the remote and inserted the DVD into the DVD player. Soon, it was playing and all four of them watched.

Johnny's interview was at the beginning of the documentary and lasted about twenty minutes. After his portion was over, her father turned it off.

"Wow, that's quite stunning," her father stated. "You seem to possess an incredible amount of knowledge about the afterlife. You have been sharing this with Julie?"

Johnny nodded. "Yes, and nineteen other people in a meetup group that I formed. I am teaching all of them about the soul, in the same way that I described in the video. We all are learning how to live by God's virtues and become more spiritually evolved. The only people I am teaching are those who are drawn to this material. I did not go to them. They came to me."

Julie's father looked at her. "Why were you drawn to this information?"

"It had to be my sister," her mother said, dejectedly.

Julie nodded. "Yes, Aunt Katie let me read her books. I learned how to soul travel a few months ago. That's when you travel outside of your body."

Everyone was silent, as Julie's parents tried to process this new information.

"Your parents say that you are a good kid," her father said to Johnny. "And that your only intent is to help humanity. Is that true?"

Johnny nodded. "Yes."

"Do you think any of your teachings could hurt Julie?" her father asked, in a calm manner.

Johnny hesitated. "I'm going to be honest with you. It's complicated. There are risks that Julie and I have taken by following this path. We are now social misfits and social outcasts. We have separated ourselves from the mainstream. The choices we have made will create problems in our lives that we will have to deal with."

Johnny paused and looked directly at her father.

"However, the path we have chosen is to be of service to humanity. We feel strongly that society is changing and that a

Chapter Eight : The Truth Shall Set You Free

spiritual answer is what people are going to be searching for. Our knowledge and understanding will benefit many, and we are here to share what we know. The genie is out of the bottle, and Julie and I are not going to change the path we have chosen. We are both going to continue living a spiritual lifestyle and increasing our spiritual knowledge. Our path is one of service to humanity."

Johnny stopped and waited for Julie's father to reply.

"I know your parents, and if they think you are following a noble path, then I am not going to condemn it. Trying to learn about the soul is not something I am interested in, but I do not judge those who do. If that is what Julie and you want to pursue, then I won't stand in your way."

Julie's mom put her hand over her eyes and did not speak.

Julie jumped up and hugged her dad. "Oh, thank you, thank you!"

Julie and Johnny walked out the front door without saying another word.

Johnny looked at Julie. "I'm not coming back for a while. I should wait until your parents have had time to adjust to this information."

"That's probably a good idea. My mom didn't look very excited about what my dad said. But she won't fight him on this. He's the boss in our household."

Johnny nodded, agreeing with her assessment of the situation. "We can spend more time at my house for a while."

Julie smiled. "Sounds good."

※ ※ ※ ※ ※

As the summer days passed, Johnny and Julie became inseparable. Every day they would get together. They would spend their time together with Julie reading books and Johnny on his laptop, blogging or surfing the Internet. At night, they would talk to each other, usually about something Julie was reading. Sometimes, they would take day trips to parks or the ocean. On Wednesday nights, which was their movie night, they would often go see a film. Both of them had abandoned their other friends. Their focus on becoming ascended masters was all they currently cared about. Their friends could not relate to this vision quest that they had begun.

"I read something that blew me away today," Julie said.

They were at Johnny's house, lying on his bed. His bedroom door was closed, but no one else was home.

"What?" Johnny asked.

"You know the line from the Bible that says that the truth shall set you free?"

Johnny nodded.

"Well, isn't that what you always talk about? Spiritual freedom and getting off the wheel of karma."

Johnny didn't reply, letting Julie explain in more detail.

"The truth is that there is only one way to become free, which is to live in accordance with God's virtues. And those virtues can only be obtained by connecting to our soul. It is when we look within and become guided from within, that those virtues manifest."

"Correct," Johnny replied. "That is the truth that can set you free. What people do not realize is that they currently are not free. Everyone is stuck on the wheel, and they have no idea that the path off the wheel is within."

"And once you look within," Julie added, "all you find is love and virtue."

"You also find out that the duality that exists on the outside world, does not exist within. When you look within, you find unity and singularity."

Chapter Eight : The Truth Shall Set You Free

Julie nodded. "Yes, you find that service to humanity and the highest good is the only option. It no longer makes sense to serve yourself, because individuality does not exist for the soul."

Johnny nodded. "Exactly. The only thing that begins to make sense is that love, compassion, and serving are the only options we have. These become the foundation of our truth, and the gateway to freedom."

"We become gentle, loving, caring, and connected to our heart-center." Julie stated.

"And committed to abiding by these virtues," Johnny added.

Julie contemplated. "It is our focus, discipline, and commitment that create the outcome. Once we integrate the truth into our mindset, our freedom is guaranteed."

"Almost," Johnny replied. "First, you have to allow the soul from within to bring awareness to your life. Once this internal guidance appears, it won't be long before your freedom is found."

"So, all we have to do is combine living with God's virtues along with inner guidance?"

Johnny nodded. "Yes, that is the truth that shall set you free."

"And the inner guidance comes from maintaining a quiet mind?" Julie asked.

"That's the starting point. First, you quiet the mind, then you wait for the soul to communicate. The soul can be felt or heard. You do this by having reverence, respect, and complete knowing that it is real. Once you open this channel, you wait for direction. If nothing comes, then you wait until it does, and trust me, at some point, it will. Once you establish communication with the soul, follow the guidance, with a deep sense of gratitude and reverence. Your integrity will manifest from your reverence."

Julie had an epiphany, and her eyes lit up. "The ego and the soul form a team, and the soul is the captain of the team."

"More like the captain of the ship," Johnny said. "What the soul says, goes. Otherwise, your life will go askew. Once you begin to live by God's virtues, you will know when a choice is not in accordance with those virtues. That will be the soul informing you to rethink that decision."

"You mean like intuition?" Julie asked.

"Yes, but it will be heightened. More intense."

Julie paused before asking her next question. "So, the communication with the soul literally begins to take over our lives? Our individuality becomes overshadowed?"

"Excellent insight," Johnny replied. "The closer we get to our soul, the further away we get from our earthly personality. We begin to change into someone else, our true self. Our focus becomes less centered on this world, and more focused on the inner reality, which is much more real."

"That's kind of scary, Johnny. I don't want to change into someone else."

"You get to decide how much you want to change. No one is going to force you. If you want, you can remain balanced, with one foot in this world and one foot in the inner world."

"What do you mean?" Julie asked.

"Currently, I live with one foot in this third dimensional reality and one foot in the fourth dimensional reality. At all times, I live with an open communication channel with my higher self, which is my soul, and my spirit guides. My consciousness is split evenly, and you cannot tell. However, if I move more of my consciousness into the fourth dimension, then my personality would likely begin to change, and I would become a different person."

"Whoa, that's fascinating," Julie said, with genuine interest. "But why would you want to become different?"

"Really for only one reason, and that would be to get closer to my soul. I could do this to get a better understanding of God's

Chapter Eight : The Truth Shall Set You Free

virtues. This might be something worth doing as an experiment. Although, it might be a mistake, because my third dimensional incarnated life is likely going to suffer."

Julie laughed. "You mean you would become a space cadet? Disconnected from this reality?"

Johnny laughed. "Yeah, something like that. I would probably stop going to school and never leave my room."

"Okay, so the key is balance?" Julie asked. "We need to open the channel to the soul, but not allow it to overwhelm us?"

Johnny nodded.

"I think I get it," Julie said. "Using the soul's guidance, we can begin to make choices that support our goal of becoming an ascended master and achieving spiritual freedom."

Johnny nodded. "Yes, we can use it for ascension, but also to create harmony in our lives. This guidance can literally expand our awareness and give us direction. We can be guided from the spiritual dimensions."

"You mean that the clearer the communication channel with our soul, the better decisions that we will make?" Julie asked.

Johnny nodded. "And our decisions should be based on following God's virtues."

"I get it," Julie said. "We should make decisions based on what we can do to help others, and for the highest good. Not what helps me as an individual. We should exclude individual satisfaction as much as possible, and focus more on humanity and the soul."

Johnny nodded. "When you are helping humanity, you are helping yourself. Conversely, when you are gratifying yourself, you are not helping humanity."

"What about going to the spa and getting a message?" Julie asked seriously.

"That's okay if it's for your health," Johnny said. "Remember, your health has a big impact on your soul frequency. If you don't take care of yourself, then your soul frequency fragments. You want to keep it as strong as possible. So, go to the spa as much as you want."

Julie smiled. "That's a relief. I love the spa!"

Johnny laughed. "Just go easy on chocolate. There are no gluttons among the ascended masters."

"What about the Buddha?" Julie asked, teasingly.

"I'm going to have to talk to him about that waistline when I get there."

Julie laughed.

* * * * *

The next day, Julie and Johnny took a drive down Highway 1 along the ocean. Their destination was the Aquarium in Monterey and to have lunch at one of Julie's favorite restaurants on Fisherman's Wharf. It was a typical summer day, with blue sky and sunshine.

"What do you know about soul visitations?" Julie asked, as she drove down the highway.

"They usually occur in the dreams of people who have lost someone close," Johnny replied. "Souls from the other side will come in our dreams to give us comfort or information."

"What about souls appearing in someone's bedroom?" Julie asked.

Johnny glanced at Julie. "Sure, that can happen. Why?"

"I was reading a blog last night about this girl who is being visited. I'm not sure if I believe it."

"Why? What did she say?"

Julie scrunched her nose. "It was gloom and doom. Pretty scary stuff."

"Such as?" Johnny asked.

Chapter Eight : The Truth Shall Set You Free

"California's supposed to become a series of tiny islands...." Julie stopped when she saw Johnny's face.

"What?" she asked, with a look of concern.

Johnny squinted his eyes and contemplated. "Don't be mad at me. There are some things that I haven't told people yet. That is one."

Julie looked at Johnny, with deep anxiety. "It's true?"

Johnny nodded. "Yeah, but it's not for at least a decade, maybe longer. And we will have plenty of warning."

"That's awful!" Julie exclaimed. "Our beautiful state is going to be submerged?"

"It's not just California, but many parts of the planet. It's an earth shift. All of the continents are going to shift. Islands and coastlines will be particularly at risk. All of Nevada, and most of Arizona and Utah will be under water. The Great Lakes will empty into the Gulf of Mexico through an inland sea."

"What is the warning before the shift?" Julie asked with concern.

"A chunk of land in Southern California will fall into the sea. It will be big enough for us to know. It will be much bigger than one mile inland, perhaps five or ten miles inland. God is going give everyone an ample warning."

Julie was quiet.

"What else was in the blog?" Johnny asked.

"I'm afraid to say," Julie said.

"Tell me," Johnny said, laughing at her fear of the future.

"Okay. She said that society is going break down and we will have to live through a very difficult period of transition. There is going to be anarchy and riots in all of the major cities. Our freedom is going to be limited, as we become a quasi-police state."

"Yes, that's true, but there is no reason to be afraid, Julie. This breakdown is actually a good thing. It is the birth pains of a new civilization. The old civilization is going to be replaced, and all of its deficiencies are going to be exposed. Anarchy and riots are symptoms of an underlying cancer that needs to be expunged. This is God's grand plan. The earth shift comes during the transition to finalize the changes."

Julie was quiet, as she contemplated. "It sounds like anarchy."

"No, quite the opposite," Johnny replied. "The rising frequencies on the planet will bring people together. There will be a recognition by the majority that we must build a new civilization, and that the old one was misaligned and irreparable. Those who try to hold on to the old ways will quickly recognize their folly. We will reach a point where everyone recognizes that we can't go back, and that we must forge ahead to build something new."

"What are you saying?" Julie asked, with concern. "That society is going to collapse?"

"No, it's going to transform," Johnny said calmly, looking at the ocean. "As long as people approach change as an opportunity, they will be able to live through the transformation with very little impact to their lives. However, those who resist change will have a very difficult time hanging on to their old way of life."

"Let me rephrase the question," Julie said somewhat sarcastically. "How far is our standard of living going to fall?"

"That's not the right question," Johnny said calmly. "If our standard of living is preventing us from living in harmony, then it's not going to fall at all. In fact, it is going to rise."

"So, from your perspective, not having cable or a smartphone is a rise in our standard of living?" Julie asked sardonically.

Johnny nodded. "If that is what it takes to live in harmony, with no crime and no corruption."

"But won't poverty rates and crime rates increase if society collapses?"

"Julie, do you really think that God spent one hundred thousand years to raise the vibration of the planet only to create poverty

Chapter Eight : The Truth Shall Set You Free

and crime? What's coming is quite the opposite. Love is coming. Harmony is coming. Unity is coming."

"Sure, but you said it would take four generations to culminate. For us, we get to endure the pain of the birth."

Johnny smiled. "But it's going to be a beautiful baby."

Julie thought about that. "Then there is nothing to worry about?"

Johnny shook his head. "No. We are lucky to be alive to witness it. We are going to witness the birth of a new civilization. One that is going to impact the entire universe in a multitude of positive ways. What is going to happen is beyond description and beyond words. Awesome is much too small a word. Perhaps, awesome times a thousand. Or wonderful times ten thousand."

"So, what you are saying is that all of the ugliness of our culture is going to be transformed into some sort of utopian society?"

Johnny nodded. "Yes, and only those souls who are advanced enough will be able to stay. Earth's time as a duality planet is quickly coming to an end. The planet is ascending to a higher frequency that no longer supports suffering, cruelty, and war."

"I'm confused," Julie said. "If we are living through a period of massive changes, then what is our role? Are we bystanders or instigators? I'm starting to get the feeling that we are becoming instigators. We can't stand on the sidelines when we know what is happening."

Johnny smiled. "I suppose there is some truth to that. We are here to help with the transition. If helping makes us instigators of change, then it is what it is. God has decided that this civilization's time must come to an end. That is why the Indigo and Crystal children are here, and that is why we are here. In fifty years, there will be very little of society that you will recognize."

"I'm not sure if I should feel happy or sad," Julie said.

"Sadness is from the ego. You should feel bliss and joy, which is from the soul."

"But it's human to feel sadness," Julie responded.

"Are you human, or are you an eternal soul?"

"I don't know," Julie said. "I think I'm both."

"You can be both, but recognize that the ego is a temporary illusion, and the soul is eternal and real. Don't let the ego trick you into thinking that it is real, or that this world is real. If you give the ego credence, then it will keep you from your soul. And remember, your soul is the only path to the truth. Without a connection to your soul, you are at the mercy of your ego, with its nefarious agenda of keeping you blocked from the truth. And the deeper the ego can block you from the truth, the more satisfaction and control the ego obtains. The more dreadful your life becomes, the more satisfied the ego becomes. So, do you want the ego to be your friend?"

"Well, I don't want to be at the mercy of the ego, so I'll be careful with that sadness stuff."

Johnny smiled. "Good girl."

Johnny looked out over the ocean as they got close to Santa Cruz. "What else did she say?"

"We begin to simplify our lives and live in small groups. People start leaving the cities and forming small communities in the middle of nowhere. Living off the grid and growing their own food."

"Yep, that's going to happen," Johnny replied.

"Will they have the Internet?" Julie asked.

Johnny nodded. "Yes, it's not going anywhere. People love the Internet and will do what it takes to keep it running. A big trend will be getting the Internet from satellites."

"She said that the economy would become hyperlocal. What did she mean?"

"Nearly everything will be obtained locally," Johnny replied, in a matter-of-fact manner. "Work, food, finances, healthcare, and

Chapter Eight : The Truth Shall Set You Free

necessities. Most of the large corporations and banks will disappear. Once the financial system changes, they will go bankrupt and close their doors."

"That's going to be messy."

"It's part of the change," Johnny said. "Many communities will be somewhat isolated, so they will need to become self-sustaining. What will be wonderful is that these communities will become experiments on how to design a sustainable, harmonious community. Many will succeed splendidly. They will become templates that other communities copy."

"That sounds good," Julie said, with a smile.

"What else?" Johnny asked.

"Blue energy. It's supposed to make oil no longer necessary."

"Ah yes, blue energy. This is free energy and what allows these new communities to thrive. The energy is collected from the air and used to convert water into hydrogen fuel cells, which is a perfectly clean energy, with the only waste product being water. The fuel cells can be used to power homes, businesses, and vehicles. It can also be used to purify water."

"I can't wait for that," Julie said.

"What else?"

"Energy healing. She made it sound like miracle healing and that there would no longer be a need for hospitals."

Johnny smiled. "Oh, this is really cool. As the frequency of the mass consciousness increases, healers will have an easier time acting as a conduit. People can be healed for just about anything using conscious energy. As long as you want to be healed and believe that you can be healed, an energy healer will be highly effective. Every community will have at least one energy healer, and often, they will be children. After the miracles start happening, no one will question their effectiveness. Soon, people will stop going to the doctor; instead, they will go to an energy healer.

"The reason why energy healing becomes effective is that our bodies are basically energy systems. An ailment is simply an energy imbalance or a misaligned frequency. As our bodies become more crystalline and vibrate at higher frequencies, it becomes much easier for energy healers to realign our frequencies. In fact, in the not too distant future, most people will no longer get sick.

"Very cool," Julie said.

"What else?"

"Extraterrestrials. She said they are going to help us."

Johnny nodded. "Yep. That's where the blue energy comes from. They also help us with our spirituality. They tell us to stop using organized religion, and that all of us are incarnated eternal souls from the same Creator. They tell us that the meaning of life is to serve the Creator and to serve one another. And that the only thing that matters is love. This has the impact of steadily eliminating war.

"People will recognize that these extraterrestrials are from all over the galaxy and come from more advanced civilizations. We accept their words as truth. What convinces people is that the extraterrestrials are from multiple star systems. There are Pleiadians, Sirians, Arcturians, Lyrians, and others. When all of these extraterrestrials say the same thing about the Creator, people will recognize the truth. Plus, the Catholic Church comes clean about Mary Magdalene, and explains that she was married to Jesus and was never a prostitute."

"So, all of the world's religions dissolve?"

Johnny nodded. "Yes, by the middle of this century, most people will be turning away from their church. By the end of this century, there will be no more religions."

"When do the extraterrestrials land?" Julie asked, with excitement.

Chapter Eight : The Truth Shall Set You Free

"Not for a while. Perhaps twenty twenty-seven, maybe later. They won't land until we have increased our vibration high enough as a civilization to accept them."

"If they landed today, people would freak out. Twenty twenty-seven seems too soon," Julie said.

"A lot will change between now and twenty twenty-seven."

Julie was quiet.

"What else?"

"That's all I remember, except for one last thing. She said that the country would begin breaking up soon."

Johnny nodded. "Yep, that's coming. Many states become new countries, and that is where people move to start their new communities. These new countries will be focused on freedom and individual liberty, which the U.S. Government has been steadily curtailing."

Julie pulled into the Aquarium parking lot.

"Good timing! We're here," Johnny said.

"Seeing the fish will be calming, after all that talk about societal collapse," Julie said.

"I love this place!" Johnny exclaimed. "Let's go see the manta rays!"

Chapter Nine

ASCENSION TRAINING

Julie honked her car horn outside of Johnny's house. It was meetup group night and she had come to pick him up. He ran down the stairs and yelled good-bye to his parents on his way out the door.

"We get to do ascension training tonight, don't we?" Julie asked, as soon as Johnny had fastened his seat belt.

"Yep. I think everyone is ready. We'll probably need more than one hour."

"That's okay. Everyone stays after anyway, except us," Julie said, glancing at Johnny as she drove.

"That's what I was thinking. We could probably do an hour and a half without anyone complaining."

"You can ask them," Julie said.

* * * * *

As usual, everyone was early, except for Johnny and Julie. When they walked in, everyone was sitting around, talking and waiting for Johnny to arrive.

"Take your places, everyone," Julie said. "Tonight, our ascension training begins."

Julie found a seat, and Johnny remained standing in front of the group.

Johnny waited for everyone to find their place. "Okay, let's begin. I want to begin the training by having as many people speak tonight as possible. Can everyone stay for an hour and a half tonight?"

Everyone was nodding and nobody said anything.

"I'll take that as a yes," Johnny said. "We are going to begin your training by teaching each other. Each of you will stand up in front of the group and explain what you are doing to become an ascended master, and how your life is changing. We will learn from each other. Okay, who wants to go first?"

"How about you?" Julie said to Johnny.

Johnny contemplated. "No, I want to go last today, so that I can add anything that's not said."

Johnny found a place to sit down.

Eric rose. "I'll go first." He found a place to stand in front of the group. "I do the hand prayer every morning after I wake up. I acknowledge that I am an eternal soul in a human body and that I am here to serve the Creator and humanity. I recognize and accept that my soul wants to manifest love, and that self-love is the starting point. However, my love of self is actually a love of my soul, which is my true self.

"Then from my love of self, I acknowledge that my purpose is to love humanity and all-that-is. My purpose is not self-gratification or selfish endeavors seeking happiness through ego gratification. My purpose is to get closer to my soul so that my awareness expands and my etheric soul becomes more luminous.

"After I acknowledge my soul and humanity, I vow to only make choices for the highest good. My goal is to keep my mind quiet and pay attention to my soul. On most days, my ego will try to get my attention by getting me to complain about my life. I will then quiet my mind and let those thoughts pass. I will stay focused on my objective of keeping my mind quiet and remaining humble, calm, compassionate, and loving.

"I have been changing and becoming a different person. No longer do I like to play computer games. Instead, I spend most of my time reading and accumulating knowledge, especially channeled material about ascension, but also information about

Chapter Nine : Ascension Training

reincarnation and Crystal children. I no longer enjoy television or small talk. If a conversation does not have any substance, I tend to get bored easily.

"My soul talks to me at least once a day. Sometimes, it can be quite dramatic. For instance, yesterday, a teacher at school told us something important and I didn't listen. I was being arrogant, but I didn't realize it. Then when I left class, I tripped and fell down. When I was falling, I could hear my soul telling me to listen to the teacher next time. I don't know how to describe it, but I knew instantly that it was my soul that made me trip. I have walked down those steps a thousand times and never once came close to falling.

"My soul started doing this whenever I stray from my commitment to adhere to God's virtues. Anything that is not in accordance with integrity and gratitude is not tolerated. Sometimes, I will hear my soul say, no. Sometimes, I will feel it. Sometimes, I will hear my name. It communicates in a variety of methods, but it is always to get my attention. I feel like I am in training, and my soul is the teacher."

Eric finally stopped.

Johnny raised his hand. "I have a few questions, but first, I want to say that what you are doing is working out incredibly well. Don't stop. You are forming a relationship with your soul, which will continue to improve. You are achieving self-realization that your soul exists. This is coming from your relationship with your soul, and by living with God's virtues. Continue to focus on love, both the love of self and the love of humanity. Tell the universe what you love, and it will be given to you. Why? Because love is congruent with the universe's objective. That's what the universe wants. Also, you are now creating and expanding a frequency of love in your life. That is the tone that you are setting, and it will now attract to you experiences that match that tone. So, my question is, can you describe your love of self?"

Eric hesitated. "It's hard to describe. It's not a narcissistic self-love. It's more of a reverence of the soul and my true self. In fact, the self-love is not for my current personality. It is much more expansive than that. It is an all-encompassing love for my complete self, of which the personality is only a part."

Johnny nodded. "Excellent. Does anyone have any questions for Eric?"

"Do you find yourself much calmer now? Almost as if everything is going in slow motion?" someone asked.

"Yeah, definitely," Eric replied, with a sense of awe. "When I'm not reading or talking to someone, I find that I like to keep my mind quiet. This allows me to remain extremely calm, no matter what is happening around me. With the soul present, I feel like I know what to do in any situation. I no longer feel alone."

"The calmness comes from tapping into the bliss of the soul," Johnny said. "The soul's natural emotion is bliss, which is a pervasive calmness. The key to both obtaining and maintaining this bliss is a connection to love, which comes from the soul. Eric, you actually did an excellent job explaining how you obtained it. Your love of self, love of humanity, and following God's virtues, opened the gateway to bliss."

"Is the ego the only thing that can block our bliss?" Julie asked.

Johnny nodded. "Yes. Definitely. The ego is our nemesis. If we keep our minds quiet, with a connection open to our soul, then we should be able to remain calm, no matter what is occurring in our lives. We can embrace uncertainty and accept anything that happens with gratitude. And since this is ascension training, you should know that the ego's favorite weapon of choice is fear. Always recognize that fear is false evidence appearing real, and that it is an illusion. In fact, fear and the truth cannot coexist, because when truth is understood, there is nothing to fear. So, instead of feeling fear, recognize that you are an eternal soul, and this life is simply a simulation. You cannot die. The worst thing that can happen is

Chapter Nine : Ascension Training

that you will experience trauma. That might not be any fun, but it will be a blessing and opportunity, which is essentially what this lifetime is all about. An opportunity to grow and evolve the soul. So, embrace uncertainty, but don't embrace fear."

Johnny looked at Eric. "Eric, thank you for sharing."

Eric sat down.

"Who wants to go next?" Johnny asked.

Julie quickly rose from her seat. "I will."

She took a few steps and then turned and faced the group.

"All this talk of loving yourself and loving humanity and following God's virtues makes me want to have a group hug. I hope all of you are as committed to this as Eric has become. I know that I am. Some of you may be jealous of me because I have been hanging out with Johnny and getting taught one on one. But you don't need to be. As Eric explained, this is up to us. In fact, Eric is more into this than me. I have been reading constantly, and I do the hand prayer every morning, but my soul has been elusive. I know it's there, because I call on it to do soul travel, but during the day, I haven't felt that calmness and bliss yet. I know it's coming, but I need to do more work.

"I did want to share something with regard to the cells in our bodies. They are changing from carbon to crystalline. Those of us who can change them to one hundred percent crystalline have the opportunity to ascend. I think all of us can do this. The key is love, because crystalline is love-based. The more we live God's virtues and the more we manifest love in our lives, the easier it is for your cells to change from carbon to crystalline.

"One last thing I wanted to share. In order to create crystalline bodies, we have to release and clear our negative karma from this life and our past lives. We may not have much negative karma from this life because we are young. However, we all have some from past lives. This can be cleared through meditation by calling in Archangel Michael and using his violet flame. This violet flame can be used for clearing and cleansing our etheric soul body. I call it in every morning when I do my hand prayer. If you surround yourself in the violet flame for a few weeks, that should do the trick."

Julie started to move toward her seat.

"Not so fast," Johnny said. "We have questions."

Julie smiled and then moved back to answer questions.

"First," Johnny asked, "we all want you to teach us how to soul travel. Can we meet somewhere tomorrow and you can teach us?"

"Sure, we can go to Castle Rock Park," Julie said. "How about one o'clock. Can everyone make it?"

Everyone nodded.

"Okay, next question," Johnny said. "You said that your soul has been elusive. I know that's not true. You hear things all of the time from your higher self or spirit guides."

"I suppose, but I don't feel the calmness Eric was talking about."

"Tell them what you hear," Johnny said.

"I get premonitions. The premonitions are usually accurate. I can be walking to class and I will know the first thing the teacher is going to say. I don't know if I hear the premonitions; it's more like a thought. I get ideas and they form very quickly. I also have visions. They can be very weird and make no sense, just like dreams, although they happen during the day when I am awake."

"The soul can communicate in a variety of ways," Johnny said. "Be open to the possibilities. I'm sure many of you are going to tell us some interesting methods. The more that everyone shares, the more the group will benefit."

"Julie, I have questions about soul travel, but I'll save them for tomorrow," someone said. "I do have one question. Do you still hang out with your friends?"

Chapter Nine : Ascension Training

Of all the people in the group, Julie was the most popular at school. She was pretty, nice, friendly, and a likable person. She had a lot of friends.

Julie hesitated. "I haven't been this summer. I'm on a vision quest, trying to expand my awareness and learn about the soul. I know that I am changing as a person. I don't know who I will hang out with next year. It might just be all of you."

"Julie, you can sit down, and thanks for sharing," Johnny said.

Julie sat down.

Johnny scanned the members. "I know that I have disrupted your lives by starting this meetup group. This disruption is likely to increase. If you want your old life back, then I recommend that you stop attending. The further you go down this rabbit hole, the less likely you will be able to turn around."

"I'm not going anywhere," Jackie said. "This is the best thing that has ever happened to me. I have angels in my room now. It's wonderful."

"Jackie, come up and share," Johnny said.

Jackie stood and found a place to address the group. "When I first started doing the hand prayer, I did it three times a day, before each meal. Now I just do it when I wake up and before I go to bed. I also do a Lemurian tone in the shower each morning. I read that toning is helpful for building our crystalline light body. And I meditate for fifteen minutes every day. When I meditate, I feel my body vibrate and make a connection with my soul. I open the gateway and let my soul fill me with love. I tell my soul, 'Thank you.'

"After about a month of doing this, an angel appeared in my room. She was beautiful. She told me, 'Thank you.' I'm not sure what she meant, but I think I'm supposed to continue my ascension training."

Jackie stopped.

"How has your life changed?" Johnny asked.

"I've changed quite a bit. I now ooze love in everything I do. I love everyone that I see, no matter what. All I feel is gentleness, compassion, and unconditional love. Those three things are what I'm committed to living at all times. I've been able to marginalize my ego almost completely. Sometimes, I feel a desire for boys, or sometimes I'll put on makeup to look pretty, but my ego is largely benign. I haven't felt anger or fear in several weeks."

"That's amazing progress," Johnny said. "Tell us more about how you achieved it."

"It all starts with the hand prayer," Jackie said seriously. "You have to make a commitment to follow it. There can't be any cheating. Like you said, we have to be in integrity and show the soul that we are committed. If you commit to serving the soul, then that is what you have to do. And you serve by following the virtues of God and living a life of integrity and gratitude. Once you adopt these, the ego has a hard time getting your attention. If you have integrity that God is all and all is love, then your choices begin to become congruent with that belief system. Perhaps the key is recognizing that we are God's emissaries and that we are here to serve the truth. That is our objective. Conversely, if we serve the ego, then we are serving a lie. In fact, separation is a lie and the ego's job is to keep us hypnotized into believing that lie.

"Once you know the truth about life, serving the truth is much easier. In fact, if you know the truth and refuse to serve, then you are essentially no different than Satan. And who wants to be Satan? I have my eye on the goal, which is to obtain self-mastery and become an ascended master. God wants us to graduate from this wheel of karma, and to do that, all we have to do is expand our awareness. That is accomplished only one way, which is spending every waking moment focused on the truth. If we do that, then our choices will always be for the highest good."

Jackie stopped.

Chapter Nine : Ascension Training

"I have a question," Johnny said. "How often do you live in the present moment?"

"Nearly all the time," Jackie replied. "It is the only way to keep the communication channel to the soul open. By keeping your mind quiet, it forces you to live in the now. And the more you keep your mind quiet, the easier it is to spot the ego trying to weasel its way into your life. I would add that, without my daily meditation, I probably wouldn't be able to keep my mind quiet. If you are not meditating, then you should start."

"Is there anything else that you would like to share?" Johnny asked.

Jackie contemplated. "I should say something about the heart-center, since it is so critical to how I now live. Don't think with your head; instead, think with your heart. When you think with your head, more often than not, you will be thinking with your ego. Use the heart and let it guide you. The soul knows the truth, and you can trust it. We should trust our feelings and follow them. That's the path of love."

Jackie sat down.

"Thanks for sharing, Jackie. Okay, who's next?"

Steven stood up and found a place in front of the group. "I'll go."

"After I do the hand prayer in the morning, I bring down the divine presence to be with me. You can call this the soul or our higher self, but I call it the divine presence. Once it is with me, we act as a team. I become a conscious instrument of the divine presence. My goal or objective is to become so closely connected to this presence that we meld into one. I am hoping that I can literally ascend off of this planet once I get close enough."

Steven paused and waited for someone to ask a question.

"Do you talk to this presence?" Johnny asked.

"Not really. I listen. I listen for guidance and for the truth to come through. They talk to me more than I talk to them. Although,

127

I suppose that when I pray, I am talking to them. But it's rarely a conversation."

"What is the truth to you?" Johnny asked.

"That we are eternal souls and that our core is love, which is pure and innocent. Our objective is to epitomize that love and make it stronger and stronger. Anything that is not of love is a lie, and should be rejected. We should serve the soul, which knows best. We do this by remaining humble at all times, and rejecting the ego's attempt at searching for happiness through experience."

"Are you saying that happiness isn't important?" Johnny asked.

"Happiness should not be an objective. It should be the result of your life. If you are not happy, then you are not living right. It should be the natural outcome of merging with your soul."

"Excellent," Johnny said. "I would have used the word integrating, but merging is the same thing. We do not need to create happiness when the soul is already naturally blissful. The ego is searching for something that we already have. All we need to do is integrate the soul into our lives, and we will feel the natural bliss that it provides. And the only thing that can rob you of that bliss is the ego's ability to block you from happiness.

"Steven, what does this divine presence tell you?" someone asked.

"When I am out of alignment with God's virtues, I will feel it. For some reason, my soul is interested in what I eat. I have begun to feel a revulsion for meat and dairy products, as well as sugar. I've lost twenty pounds and I feel much better. Also, I can't play very many video games anymore. I don't think my soul likes the violence."

Several people laughed.

"Also, my soul doesn't like it when I judge other people. If I say something mean to someone, I feel like I did something really bad. My soul has been training me to think like it thinks."

Chapter Nine : Ascension Training

"Excellent," Johnny said. "This is literally how we obtain self-mastery, which leads to ascension. Once the soul begins to train us, we are on our way to success. The first step is inviting the soul into our life by marginalizing the ego with a quiet mind and following God's virtues. The second step is paying attention to the soul once it appears. If we are lucky, it will teach us self-mastery. It will be our teacher."

Johnny stood and faced the group.

"This is a two-way process. First, we have to make a commitment that we are ready to follow God's virtues and to serve the soul. Second, we have to do what the soul tells us. If the soul says to stop eating meat, then do what it says. If the soul says to stop judging others, then stop. If we ignore what the soul is trying to teach us, then self-mastery is not possible, and the lessons will cease.

"Self-mastery is extremely difficult to achieve, because not only will the ego try to prevent us from succeeding, but the soul will often be extremely subtle in its guidance. If we are not paying close enough attention, we can easily miss an important lesson. For this reason, I recommend using a journal and writing down any potential lessons that you think the soul recommended you learn. Also, it is a good idea to review each day for important lessons."

"Steven, is there anything else that you want to share?" Johnny asked.

"Gratitude and humility. Make sure to live those virtues daily. Also, have respect and empathy for others. It's important that we respect everyone's journey. The only blasphemy is the denial of the divine, which occurs when we see someone or something as separate from ourselves. We are all one, and we need to recognize that."

Steven sat down.

Johnny remained standing. "Okay, I'll go last. I want to thank everyone for sharing tonight. I think everyone has learned an incredible amount of information through hearing from others.

For those who didn't get a chance to share, we will be doing this for the next few meetups until everyone has a chance. After that, anyone can share, if they feel compelled.

"I want to start with my morning routine. The first thing that I do is say the Lord's Prayer. I do this to show my reverence for God. The next thing that I do is sing, not words but tones. You can use your voice to vibrate your entire body. This is as good for you as meditating. After I sing and tone, I call in my spirit guides and begin the hand prayer. I start with my thumb. I say, 'Who do I serve? My ego or my soul.' I answer, 'I serve my soul. I serve the Creator. I serve humanity. I serve my true self. My soul contract is to serve the truth, and not the ego.'

"Next, I do my index finger. I say, 'Will I be prideful or grateful today? I will be grateful, and I live with gratitude and not self-indulgence. I will not allow pride to permit my ego to distract me from my objective of living God's virtues and increasing my soul frequency. Instead, I will use gratitude as a powerful virtue that allows love to flow in my life and my heart-center to remain open at all times.'

"Next, I do my middle finger. I say, 'How will I serve the soul today? With integrity and virtue. I will serve by following the virtues of God. I will be selfless and compassionate, with profound respect for all.'

"Next, I do my ring finger. I say, 'How will I follow God's virtues today? By opening my heart-center and connecting with my spirit. I will walk in love and trust. I will be guided with truth and wisdom. I will trust where I am led and understand that there is reason and meaning for where I am led. I can trust my heart, but not my head. The heart is my guiding light and will take me where I need to be. I can trust God's plan and God's perfection.'

"Next, I do my pinky. I say, 'How can I stay in my heart-center today? By remaining humble and walking with humility. By staying

Chapter Nine : Ascension Training

calm, gentle, compassionate, empathetic, and loving. If I stay in this energy, I will stay close to my heart.'

"Next, I say, 'I am, we are, and God is.' While I say this, I visualize my body surrounded in white light. Then I visualize the entire planet connected consciously. When I do this final visualization, I feel a powerful reverence and respect for the Creator and a deep sense of humility.

"Next, I bow my head and say, 'Namaste,' in case there are any spirit guides in the room with me.

"That's it. That's my morning ritual. Then I try to live my day with as much harmony and peace as possible. I try to live in the present moment, connected to my heart-center, living God's virtues. If something happens that disrupts this peace, then I try to remain calm, and understand where the disruption came from. I do everything that I can not to allow the ego to use this disruption to take away my peace.

"Each day is spent with the objective of increasing my soul vibration. This can only be achieved one day at a time, or one moment at a time. I meditate in the morning for ten minutes every day. I use this mediation to re-instill the morning hand prayer and create momentum for the rest of the day, to remain heart-centered. If anything happened the previous day that was disruptive, I can use the meditation to clear that energy."

Johnny paused and waited for any questions.

"Do you do anything else besides the hand prayer and meditation for your spiritual work?" someone asked.

"I go to the gym three times a week. I find that exercise helps me to relax and helps me to have a better relationship with my body. It's also good for my health."

"What do you do for fun?" someone asked.

"For someone on a spiritual path, fun stands for false understanding of now. The more you seek out fun, the more opportunities the ego has to disrupt your spiritual path. This is why the path of the spiritual warrior is not easy. We are at war with our ego, and we do not have the luxury of playtime. If you want to raise your soul vibration, then you have to do the soul work. And if you want to become an ascended master and obtain self-mastery, then there is not much fun and games. It's a serious task that requires commitment, discipline, and focus. It is not easy to achieve, but it can be done by those who give it their all."

"What about dancing and romance?" someone asked.

"I don't do those for fun," Johnny replied. "That's just living your life."

"Thank goodness," a girl said.

Several people laughed.

"The key is how you approach them," Johnny said. "Do you experience them for self-gratification or self-realization? If you are doing them for the latter, then it is fine. The key is not letting the ego lead your life."

Johnny looked at the clock on his phone. "Okay, time is up. We'll do this again next month. I hope everyone listens to the recording and takes notes. There was a lot of excellent information shared tonight."

Johnny and Julie walked out together. They were the first to leave.

"That was amazing, listening to people share," Julie said, as they walked to her car. "I can't wait to hear more people tell their stories."

"In a couple of years, this group is going to be incredibly aware," Johnny said. "I'm not sure what we will do, but somehow, we will need to share this with others."

"We can do a documentary, or you can continue to post on your website. Don't worry, we will think of something. The important thing now is that we all raise our vibration and obtain self-mastery."

Johnny smiled. "I like the way you think."

Chapter Ten

OUR MINDSET-THE FINAL STEP TO ASCENSION

After a few months, Johnny knew something was wrong. Several members of the meetup group seemed to be stuck. They were doing the hand prayer each morning, but it wasn't enough. He knew that something else was needed. Finally, he had an epiphany. When it came to him, he started laughing because it was so obvious. He couldn't believe that he had missed it. He was in class and started laughing at an inappropriate time during a lecture. The teacher gave him a dire look and he became silent like the rest of the class.

Once class was over, he could hardly wait for the school day to end so that he could share his insights with Julie. They had remained boyfriend and girlfriend throughout the first half of the school year. Their relationship only seemed to become stronger as the days passed. They were beginning to feel that they were soul mates who were destined to remain together.

After the last class, Johnny practically ran to Julie's car to wait for her. Once she arrived, he blurted out that they had to talk.

"Sure, where do you want to go?" Julie asked.

"Your house is good," he replied.

They got into her car and headed out of the parking lot, along with many of the other students who were leaving school.

"What is it?" Julie asked.

"I finally figured out the problem," Johnny said excitedly.

"What problem?" Julie glanced at Johnny.

"It's the most important thing, and I missed it."

"What?"

"Our mindset. Our state of mind."

"Our mindset? You're not making any sense today."

"Let's wait until we get to your house," Johnny said.

Julie pulled in to her parent's large oval driveway. She used her electronic key to open the front door, which also disabled the alarm. They went upstairs and into Julie's room.

Julie dropped her school bag on her desk and turned to Johnny. "Do you want something to eat?"

"No, I'm not hungry."

"I'll be back, I'm going to get something in the kitchen."

Johnny laid down on Julie's bed and waited for her. His mind was in overdrive, wanting to explain what he had discovered.

Julie came back with a bowl of strawberries and sat down on the bed.

"Okay, what's this most important thing?" Julie asked.

"The hand prayer has a gap in it. Somehow I missed the most important thing, which is our mindset, which is what directs us moment to moment. When Seth said that our beliefs create our reality, he was talking about our mindset. And we can decide which beliefs are in our mindset at any moment in time. And since everything happens in the present moment, how we filter our mindset is crucial to how we create our reality."

"I'm not following," Julie said, taking another bite of her strawberries.

"For instance, when we interact with others, we have to exude God's virtues. Our eye contact, body language, and words all must be in integrity. Not only that, but we must encapsulate this integrity into every word we speak and every thought we hold. Moreover, our emotions and body language must be in alignment with God's virtues. This is difficult to do because it requires a commitment to be of service to humanity and the Creator at all times."

Chapter Ten : Our Mindset-The Final Step to Ascension

"Okay, now I'm starting to get it," Julie replied. "When we communicate with others, we should do it with a mindset of love and compassion."

Johnny nodded. "Yeah, but it's more than that. Filtering our mindset to continuously be in alignment with God's virtues allows us to interact with both the outer world and the inner world with a high degree of integrity. This is done by only allowing God's virtues to filter in and out of our consciousness."

"You're losing me again," Julie said.

"Think of our mindset, our thoughts, as holy ground. We want to aspire to be pure souls that exude God's virtues. Well, we have to stop aspiring and simply do it. This can only be done by filtering our mindset to only convey God's virtues to others. This is what Buddhism calls right thought, or right thinking. We have to learn how to think better."

"Okay, I'm following," Julie said. "Basically, you are saying that our mindset is crucial to living God's virtues. And that we have to consciously be aware of what we let in and out of our consciousness. We have to walk the talk."

"Yeah, and being in integrity at all times is crucial to our success. All of God's virtues, such as purity, innocence, compassion, service, kindness, cooperation, tolerance, patience, consideration, humility, generosity, empathy, sympathy, respect, admiration, non-judgment, gratitude, honesty, trust, and unconditional love. All of these must be followed at all times to be in integrity with God's virtues."

"So, you are implying that we need a mindset that only encapsulates these virtues?" Julie asked. "And that once we begin living with this mindset, our interactions with others will change for the better?"

Johnny nodded. "That's what is missing. We need to do it more consciously."

Julie was quiet while she finished her strawberries. "That makes sense. I like it."

Johnny smiled. "I can't wait to share this at the next meetup."

"Don't get too excited. This won't be easy to achieve. We will have to keep out all of the garbage from our current mindset and become walking saints who love ourselves and humanity unconditionally at all times."

Johnny hesitated. "It's the only way we can succeed. The only way to consistently make godly choices is to love and respect yourself, as well as humanity, to the highest degree. If you do not respect yourself, or respect others for who they truly are, which is embodied Gods, then you are trapped by the ego. If we respect ourselves enough, then we can live these virtues at all times. That is the path to ascension."

"I don't believe that is the only way," Julie said. "Perhaps your way will work, but there are other ways. It's possible that these other ways are much easier. We don't necessarily have to become walking saints at all times. We are human, after all."

Johnny was quiet. "Yeah, I can't argue your point. Ascension and spiritual evolvement are a mystery. We are trying to do something that few have done before. There is not exactly a list of instructions."

* * * * *

At the next meetup group, Johnny was excited to add another element to their ascended master training regimen. As usual, when Johnny and Julie arrived, the other eighteen members were already there, waiting expectantly.

Julie found a seat and Johnny remained standing. Everyone became quiet waiting for Johnny to announce tonight's topic.

Johnny grinned. "I have good news. I recently had an epiphany that can help us with our goal of becoming an ascended master.

Chapter Ten : Our Mindset-The Final Step to Ascension

The hand prayer is a training tool to learn to live God's virtues, and how to find and communicate with our soul. However, at some point, we have to take off the training wheels and live them. In fact, the very key to being an ascended master is to walk the walk of integrity.

"It will be difficult, but it is achievable. What is required is that your mindset only allows God's virtues into your life. Every moment of your life is spent focused on your intent. Mine is to expand my spiritual awareness and to help humanity. I achieve this by living God's virtues.

"I am already living my intent, but not continuously, and not all of the time. My mindset, or present moment consciousness, constantly veers off this objective. The epiphany I had was that we have to do this continuously. Our mindset, our thoughts, need to be constantly focused on our intent. If we waver, then our integrity will also waver.

"The key to becoming an ascended master is living with integrity while serving God and humanity. This means that we must live God's virtues at all times. When we are not in alignment with God's virtues, then we have lost our integrity. I thought that I was in integrity, but then I realized that when I interact with other people, my mindset was not completely in alignment with these virtues. My eye contact, body language, words, and emotions were not in complete alignment with these virtues.

"What I realized is that I was not living who I wanted to be. It wasn't because I didn't want to live it, but because I was not consciously trying to do it. All I had to do was change my mindset and live those virtues. My identity had to change from being Johnny to being my true self. At first, this is not easy, but over time it's possible to live the virtues that you want to be. The hardest part is recognizing that everything is a mirror of yourself and that what you are seeing is really you as a different fractal of the Creator."

Johnny paused. "Does this make sense?"

"You want us to become our true self. You want the soul to manifest on earth," Jackie said.

"And to exude these virtues when we interact with others, no matter if they are family, friends, or strangers," Eric added.

"Are you asking us to love everyone equally?" Sarah asked.

Johnny nodded. "Yes. You don't get to choose who you love. Instead, you get to love everyone. Remember, the soul evolves through self-respect and self-love for yourself, and all of humanity. We have to recognize who we are and who everyone is, which are embodiments of God.

"So, yes, you love all equally, because we are all one. However, you can like your friends and family more if you want. You can have special emotional bonds with your favorite souls."

"Now I'm confused," Andy said.

"Me too," Steven added.

Johnny raised his hand to calm everyone down. "You love humanity because everyone is part of you. This love is unconditional. This is one of God's virtues and something we need to embody.

"Love is not necessarily always emotional. It can simply be a recognition of our connection to one another. Love is a form or respect, recognition. For this reason, if you love someone, you don't need to like them. If you know an evil person, you do not need to like them, but you can still love them as being part of you and part of God."

"Ugh!" Julie said.

"So, this mindset that you want us to hold at all times is supposed to love everyone equally?" Jackie asked.

Johnny nodded. "Perhaps a better word is respect. Love is more of an acknowledgment of an emotional bond to one another. When you respect all souls deeply, you can then exude that respect to all equally.

Chapter Ten : Our Mindset-The Final Step to Ascension

"The point I am really making about holding this mindset at all times, is to form a new identity. It is an identity that no longer acknowledges the lie of separation, and instead embraces the oneness of life."

"What about all of the evil in the world?" Andy asked. "And all of those who have no respect for others, such as criminals, or those who harbor ill-will towards others?"

"The only sin is the denial of the divine," Johnny replied. "It's an ego trap to label or judge others. In fact, it is judgment that keeps us from living with a mindset of God's virtues. We have to walk in God's shoes to evolve and ascend. Those shoes have been clearly defined and we know what they hold. God loves everyone unconditionally and so must we. Again, I repeat, we do not have to like everyone, and we can like people any way that we want. This is where emotion comes into play. We can have stronger emotions with those we have a strong affinity."

"But, if I don't like someone, aren't I judging them?" Jackie asked.

"Not necessarily," Johnny replied. "All of us have to choose who our friends will be. This does not mean that we are judging others because they are not in our circle of friends. It is more of a recognition of what we each need. The key is how you perceive people. If you judge others as lesser souls than yourself, then yes, that is judgment. But if you simply view them as on their own journey which does not coincide with your own, then that is fine."

"I get it!" Julie exclaimed. "Judgment is simply thinking you are better than another soul. And that runs counter to the truth, which is that we are all eternal souls on a path to enlightenment."

Johnny nodded, and everyone else was silent.

"I think I can do it," Jackie said.

"I think all of us can do it," Johnny replied. "It will take some work and a lot of practice, but we can all live these virtues by changing our mindset."

"Love is natural, but like is learned," Jackie said.

"That is what we have lost," Johnny replied. "People think that love is learned, but they are confused. Love is the natural recognition that we are one."

"We perceive separation from one another when it does not exist," Steven added.

"That is the basis of judgment and condemnation," Eric added.

"To save humanity, we have to expose the truth," Andy added.

Johnny nodded. "This is why it is so important that we begin to live these virtues and become living examples. I feel it in my bones that we have been called to do this. All we have to do is change our mindset and begin walking in God's shoes."

Johnny paused and scanned the room. "Who else thinks they can do it?"

One by one, everyone raised their hands.

Johnny smiled. "Excellent! Let's do our part to change the world. I'll see everyone next month, and we can each talk about how we have changed our mindset and our identity. It should be very interesting and useful sharing."

As Julie and Johnny walked out of the room, there was a buzz of energy. They all realized that something significant had just happened. In fact, their lives had just changed in a very positive way. Little did they know, but they had just made a pact to become ascended masters.

※ ※ ※ ※

At the next meetup group, Eric had something that he wanted to share. After everyone arrived and was seated, Eric stood and faced the gathering. He had a stack of papers in his hand.

Chapter Ten : Our Mindset-The Final Step to Ascension

"I've been working on what Johnny talked about in our last meeting. The only way I could do it was to write down my own steps. So, I wanted to share them with you."

He stepped forward and handed the stack to someone, keeping one sheet for himself. "Please pass them around. It fits on a single sheet. I call it Team Creator, and anyone who wants to join the team has to follow four steps."

Eric moved back in front of the group and waited until everyone had a sheet of paper. He read aloud.

"Step number one is intent. Everything begins with our intent. This is our mindset, our objective. It creates our motivation and desires. My intent is two-fold. First, to raise my soul vibration and increase my spiritual awareness by living God's virtues. Second, to help humanity and make the world a better place. I plan to accomplish this through my thoughts, choices, and actions.

"Step number two is our thoughts, which manifest from our beliefs. Good thoughts lead to good choices. All thoughts stem from intent and beliefs.

"Step number three is our choices. Good choices lead to good actions. All choices stem from intent, thoughts, and beliefs.

"Step number four is our actions. If an action is not in integrity with God's virtues, then you have to review your intent, thoughts, and beliefs.

"Our actions are our daily experiences. This is how we live God's virtues. Each morning I review God's virtues, and then I try to live each minute with them in my mindset. Here is the list:

Purity / Innocence

Integrity / Virtue

Grateful / Humble

Compassion / Consideration

Service / Generosity

Sympathy / Empathy

Kindness / Friendliness
Patience / Tolerance
Peace / Joy
Non-attachment / Selfless
Surrender / Egoless

"During the day, we can identify any actions that fail to follow God's virtues using this list:

Me instead of we.
Temptation instead of innocence.
Desire instead of contentment.
Head instead of heart.
Busy mind instead of quiet mind.
Judgment instead of unconditional love.
Harshness instead of forgiveness.
My Happiness instead of Our Happiness
Taker instead of giver.
Selfish instead of selfless.
Prideful instead of grateful.
Narcissist instead of in service.
Hedonist instead of simple living.

"These lists help me to maintain my intent. Also, as a member of Team Creator, I constantly remember throughout the day the four steps for membership: Intent, Thoughts, Choices, and Actions. If any thoughts, choices, or actions are misguided, then I refer back to my intent. As a member of Team Creator, I have this code that must be followed at all times. This is how I live day to day.

"What makes this list so useful, is that if you we can analyze our intent on a daily basis and steadily refine it until we have reached our goal of zero misguided choices."

Eric stopped, and the room was silent.

Chapter Ten : Our Mindset-The Final Step to Ascension

"This is really cool, Eric," Johnny said. "Can I add this to my webpage and ask people to join Team Creator?"

Eric nodded. "Sure, that would be great."

"I think we should all join Team Creator," Julie said excitedly. "Let's start a movement, Youtube videos and all."

Everyone was smiling and laughing.

"Yeah!" Jackie yelled. "Let's do it."

* * * * *

It wasn't long before the Team Creator Youtube channel had ten thousand followers. Someone from the group posted a short video nearly every day that everyone who was on Team Creator could watch. What started out as a meetup group to become ascended masters had evolved into a movement to make the world a better place. Team Creator was a group of people dedicated to serving both the Creator and humanity. Simultaneously they were evolving spiritually to become ascended masters.

The following summer they decided to have a large meetup for all members of Team Creator at Castle Rock Park. They had no idea how many people would show up or how they would pay for it. After a couple of weeks of planning, they were able to accumulate two thousand dollars. This was spent on food and drinks, but they asked people to bring their own just in case there was a big turnout.

About five hundred people from all over the United States showed up. It was a diverse group of all ages and all ethnic backgrounds. Everyone was in their element and completely at peace. It was a family of like-minded people.

The weather was beautiful with a clear blue sky and a very light cool breeze.

Johnny had a small stage erected, along with a microphone and speaker system. For several hours people were given the opportunity to tell their stories and share what it was like for them to be part of Team Creator. If you wanted to speak, you had to request a number from one of the organizers, who were dressed in blue tee shirts that said Team Creator across the front. Johnny put all of the numbers into a bowl and then pulled one out to see who would speak next.

Once the short lectures began, everyone gathered around the stage to listen. They were like children at Disneyland, excited to be there. Everyone wanted to hear each other's stories.

Johnny reached into the bowl and then announced, "Number twenty-three is first. Please keep your comments to fifteen minutes or less so that everyone has a chance to speak. If you hear the bell, then your time is up."

The first speaker was a girl in her twenties that was all smiles. "I'm Lori! And I couldn't be more happy to be here among my family. I joined Team Creator about three months ago, and my life has completely changed for the better. I always knew that there was a way to serve both humanity and my spirit. There is a saying that the only way to change humanity is to change yourself. I believe that.

"When we shine our light, we put out the darkness. As Team Creator we are all shining lights slowly putting out the darkness. The evil and darkness that pervades humanity at this time is coming to an end. The pervasive crime, violence, and ill-will is ending because of what we have started. The love that we are manifesting is a force that cannot be stopped. The truth of who we are is coming out. We are all embodiments of God, the Creator. I love all of you. Thanks!"

The crowd roared their approval as Lori handed the microphone to Johnny and stepped off the stage. He reached into the bowl. "Number nine is next."

Chapter Ten : Our Mindset-The Final Step to Ascension

A man in his fifties jumped onto the stage. "I don't know if fifteen minutes is going to be enough for me. I have a lot to say. My name is Kevin and I'm from Bend, Oregon. I've been a member of Team Creator for several months, after my daughter emailed me excitedly about this new movement. She is a newage millennial, and she has always craved the ideals that Team Creator espouses. Like many of you, she was disappointed by the direction of humanity and the lack of a voice that she had. She felt powerless to politicians and corporations.

"I shared with her newage metaphysics and hoped that would be a sufficient outlet for her despair. It was not sufficient until she found Team Creator. Now she is a new person. She lives each day with a zest that was not there before. We see each other nearly every day and remind ourselves of the four steps to being on Team Creator. She verbalizes God's virtues aloud in reverence and never lets me forget my intent.

"Do you want to meet her?" Kevin asked the crowd.

Cheers of yes reverberated throughout the crowd. Kevin waved for his daughter to join him on the stage.

"Her she is, Kelly!" Kevin waited for Kelly to hop up onto the stage and handed her the microphone.

The crowd roared their approval.

Kelly waved to the crowd, holding her number up high. "I'll wait my turn. I have a number too!"

She gave Kevin back the microphone and hopped back down off the stage. The crowd applauded.

Kevin addressed the crowd. "I've been reading metaphysics and newage literature for over twenty years. I've always kept to myself and thought spirituality was something we did on our own. This is the first time I've been at a gathering with other newage people, and it feels great to be here. I've always known that we newagers espouse the future of humanity, but I never expected a movement to arise that reveals the truth to the world. At least not in my lifetime.

"Lori said that we can only change the world by changing ourselves. I agree with her. The light on the planet increases one soul at a time. Eventually, we will reach critical mass and the Creator will wave his hand over humanity, and it will change in a blink of the eye. Once we adequately inform the Creator that we are tired of the inhumanity, and that we desire peace and love, we shall have it. The idea that human nature will always lead to war and conflict is pure nonsense. It doesn't have to be this way."

The bell sounded and Kevin handed his microphone to Johnny. The crowd roared their approval and applauded strongly.

For the next few hours, one person after another came up and told their story of why they were now a member of Team Creator. It was a beautiful confirmation for all those in attendance. It revealed that what they were pursuing had support. They were not doing this alone.

The last person to speak was Johnny.

"I get to speak last. My name is Johnny. From my blue tee shirt, you can see that I'm one of the organizers and one of those who started Team Creator. Most of you don't know this, but Team Creator arose from a group of teenagers who formed a local meetup group to become ascended masters.

"What you don't realize is that by being part of Team Creator, you are actually an ascended master in training. The development and evolvement of your soul from being part of Team Creator cannot be more sublime. Those who become ascended masters literally have the freedom to direct their own soul development. It is the ultimate goal for a soul. It is the ultimate objective.

"Kelly said earlier that she knew that she was on this planet to create something wonderful for future generations. That is true, but what is also true is that we are creating our own soul's future. By being a member of Team Creator, you get two benefits. The first

Chapter Ten : Our Mindset-The Final Step to Ascension

is the opportunity to help humanity and the future of humanity. The second is the opportunity to evolve your soul and the future of your soul. Do not take either of these for granted or lightly, and remember to follow the code: Intent, Thoughts, Choices, and Actions. Keep peace and joy in your heart, but also the fortitude and determination to remain part of Team Creator.

"I have one last request. I would like everyone to help us to post videos on our Team Creator Youtube channel. Send us an email, and we will give you access to upload videos. Let's see how big a team we can create."

Johnny smiled as he looked out over the crowd. "Enjoy the rest of the day and let's do this again next year."

All of the organizers were sitting together in their blue tee shirts near the stage listening to Johnny. These were the original nineteen members of the ascended masters meetup group. As Johnny stepped off the stage, they all rose and gave Johnny a group hug. It was their way of celebrating a victory of sorts.

After the group hug, they walked back to where they had set up tables and sat down to eat and share each other's company. People from other tables came over to meet them and visit. Many of them were adults who were amazed at the maturity of these young teenagers.

"Where are the adults?" Someone asked.

Julie laughed and pointed at Johnny. "He's our adult."

"You mean to tell me that you all you kids created Team Creator? There was no adult input?" The same gentleman asked.

Johnny smiled. "Just like the Bible says, 'and the children shall lead them.'"

Everyone smiled.

www.ingramcontent.com/pod-product-compliance
Lightning Source LLC
Chambersburg PA
CBHW070621300426
44113CB00010B/1611